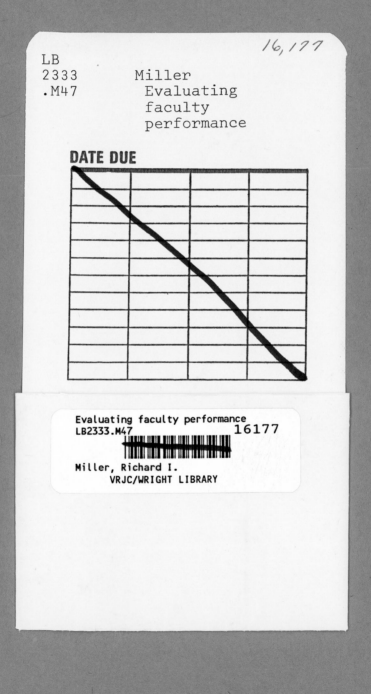

Evaluating Faculty Performance

Richard I. Miller

EVALUATING FACULTY PERFORMANCE

Jossey-Bass Publishers

San Francisco · Washington · London · 1974

EVALUATING FACULTY PERFORMANCE
by Richard I. Miller

Copyright © 1974 by: Jossey-Bass, Inc., Publishers
615 Montgomery Street
San Francisco, California 94111
&
Jossey-Bass Limited
3 Henrietta Street
London WC2E 8LU

Library of Congress Catalogue Card Number LC 70-184958

International Standard Book Number ISBN 0-87589-123-3

Manufactured in the United States of America

JACKET DESIGN BY WILLI BAUM

FIRST EDITION
First Printing: March 1972
Second Printing: April 1972
Third Printing: August 1972
Fourth Printing: March 1974

Code 7204

The Jossey-Bass
Series in Higher Education

Preface

$\mathcal{T}$he crisis in higher education has many sources: the war in Vietnam, racial tensions, the continuing conflict between science and humanism, and a financial drouth. Within the higher education system itself, the lack of defined ends and a management crisis further complicate the situation. Many colleges and universities retain antiquated administrative procedures, and their faculties have not come to grips with self-discipline and effective management. Reflecting these inadequacies, faculty evaluation is one important and sensitive problem that is seldom confronted directly. The "band-aid" approach, which too often characterizes attempts to deal with this problem, needs to be replaced by an articulated procedure in which the key concepts are individualization, flexibility (with joint planning to achieve these aims), comprehensiveness, and self-evaluation. The procedure which has been presented in this volume applies modern concepts of evaluation in which feedback and guidance are as important as judgment.

The study which was the precursor of this book was begun in August 1968 as a project of Committee "C" of the University of Kentucky chapter of the American Association of University Professors. Members of this committee were: Richard I. Miller, chairman; Lewis Donohew, associate professor of journalism; Louis Karmel, associate professor of educational psychology and counseling; Raymond Smith, associate professor of theater arts; Donald

Spicer, assistant professor of mathematics; Norman Taylor, professor of agronomy; and Harwin Voss, professor of sociology. The committee met with the deans and key administrative officials of the university, and an "outside" search, undertaken by myself, included visits to several well-known sources of materials on higher education such as the Center for Research and Development in Higher Education (Berkeley) and the national associations in Washington, D.C. An annotated bibliography was prepared by Terry Leigh, a graduate student.

Building upon the Committee "C" work, which included the sections in this book on basic assumptions and operational principles, I developed the operational and weighing procedures without benefit of committee criticism and suggestions because of the pressures of time and the change in professional positions. As the result of a study by the Liaison Committee at Baldwin-Wallace College in early 1970, some changes were made in basic procedure. Members of the committee were: Roger Stansfield, professor of chemistry (chairman); Grayson Lappert, professor and department head of English; David Proctor, professor and department head of physics and chairman of the Division of Science and Mathematics; James Ross, professor and department head of speech and theater arts; and Kenneth Whelan, associate professor of psychology. A special subcommittee included John Heter, associate professor of education; Sherwin Iverson, assistant professor of philosophy; and James Nuss, associate professor of chemistry. Another Baldwin-Wallace committee undertook a study of faculty evaluation and developed a different overall approach while retaining the basic instrument for student appraisal of instruction. Research on the student appraisal instrument was done by Stephen L. Whiteman, associate professor of psychology, and committee chairman.

My family has been particularly supportive of the many evening and morning hours spent on this project, and I am sincerely appreciative of my wife, Peggy's, understanding and assistance. Joan, Diane, and Janine helped me keep a sense of proportion with their reactions at various stages of the project.

I acknowledge with deep gratitude these individuals and

Preface

others who have contributed some part in developing this procedure.
Yet I take full responsibility for the contents herein, somewhat in the
spirit of Sir Thomas More as he approached the scaffold for his
execution. Turning to the executioner, he said: "Assist me up, and
in coming down, I will shift for myself."

Berea, Ohio   RICHARD I. MILLER
January 1972

Contents

xiii

Contents

Appraisal Forms

Evaluating Faculty Performance

Faculty
Evaluation

ଈୖୢୖଈୢୖୖଈୢୖୖଈୢୖୖଈୢୖୖଈୢୖୖଈୢୖୖଈୢୖୖଈ

*L*ogan Wilson, former president of the University of Texas, wrote over twenty-five years ago in *The Academic Man:* "Indeed, it is no exaggeration to say that the most critical problem confronted in the social organization of any university is the proper evaluation of faculty services, and giving due recognition through the impartial assignment of status" (1942, p. 112).* Today, faculty evaluation remains one of the most complex aspects of the academic world. Fiscal pressures on public and private colleges alike are forcing them to find ways of determining effectiveness and efficiency— which means evaluation. The problem is further complicated by the expanding size of public colleges and universities, the increasingly varied assignments undertaken by academic personnel, and the building pressures for organizational and instructional change in higher education.

This book endeavors to provide a comprehensive, sensitive, sensible, systematic, and manageable approach to the improvement of academic performance through faculty evaluation. Aware of the

* Complete citations for all references can be found in the Bibliography. In the text, only authors' names and years of publication are given.

1

controversies and difficulties surrounding the subject, I believe that evaluation procedures are too important to be developed by default and too sensitive to be developed by those outside academic life. It is too easy for those who possess a passing knowledge of higher education and generalizations about inefficiency and waste to computerize people and programs, elevating quantification at the expense of the teaching-learning process. The basic guideline should be quality—what happens to the student in the classroom. We do need quantifiable data, but we also need to recognize and act upon their limitations in terms of what we are seeking to develop—a competent, sensitive, effective, humane person. At the same time we need to recognize and respect the advances that have been and are being made in measurement. This book is based on the hopeful premise that these measures can be applied with optimum flexibility, artistry, individualization, and wisdom.

The first chapter develops the basic assumptions and operational principles for the remainder of the book. One needs to be clear on basic assumptions before proceeding, and the process of definition may be quite time-consuming. To skip over this task or take it lightly may lead to compounded problems later. Everything that eventually becomes operational should relate to basic assumptions. The heart of the book, however, is the second chapter. Classroom teaching for the large majority of colleges and universities is the reason for their existence and therefore deserves the special attention given it in this chapter.

The eight remaining operational categories discussed in Chapter Three represent, for some professors, aspects of their professional responsibility more significant than classroom teaching. The approach, therefore, stresses the importance of tailoring the professional responsibilities of the individual faculty member, insofar as it is feasible, along the lines of his interests and talents.

The reader will find that a quantified, one-page evaluation form has been developed for each of the nine categories as well as for the activities within these categories. The appraisal instrument for classroom teaching has been researched; the other forms have

2

been analyzed, used, and modified several times but research on them is not yet available.

The final chapter provides a method of arriving at decisions on performance. Also included is a discussion of the questions and issues which pertain to faculty evaluation and weigh so significantly upon its implementation. I expect that no college or university will wholly adopt the approach detailed in this book. I would hope that the philosophy, procedures, and substance would be eclectically chosen and modified to suit the uniqueness on any particular campus.

Chapter 1

Basic Assumptions and Operational Procedures

$\mathscr{A}$ ny effort to introduce a system of faculty evaluation should seriously consider beginning with formulation of basic assumptions. What can be agreed upon? In some cases it may be precious little, but this circumstance should be learned early, when some attitudinal alterations still may be possible, rather than after the evaluation procedure itself has been developed.

BASIC ASSUMPTIONS

The procedure suggested here proceeds from six assumptions concerning evaluation. National rather than local in scope, their applicability to the local campus is, to some extent, dependent on local issues. As reflections of national trends in faculty evaluation, however, they may merit the attention of all those concerned with the improvement of present methods for faculty evaluation.

The trend toward accountability. Colleges and universities can be expected to become increasingly conscious of cost-effectiveness and cost-benefit procedures in the seventies. Taxpayers, trustees, and donors have a right to expect more efficient management of institutions of higher education than is now present in many in-

4

stances, and the severe economic conditions demand it. Speaking at the annual conference of the American Association for Higher Education, Kerr (1971) said: "Cost-effectiveness of operations will be more carefully examined. If this is not done internally, it will be done externally by the new experts working for legislatures and governors." Accountability is a basic consideration in effective management, and an important area of application is faculty performance. Since accountability requires some precision and a systematic means of gathering, analyzing, and evaluating data, demands for improved methods of evaluating college faculty will be forthcoming.

Merit evaluation preferable. Since about 1968, the national associations and organizations advocating a civil service approach to professors' salaries have made significant inroads into the merit concept, largely because these forces are well organized and experienced in the skills of negotiation; also the economic recession has tightened the professorial job market and made job security a more dominant issue than it was during previous years when collegiate affluence allowed greater professional mobility. College faculty members, furthermore, tend to be inexperienced and disinterested in the negotiation process. Most professors, for example, do not know or consider what they may be giving up in the collective bargaining process.

The across-the-board increase, the civil service or union concept, is based upon the assumption that faculty members are professionals who perform at optimum efficiency. Their years of service and rank, then, become the bases for awarding salary increases. Furthermore, there are the assumptions that faculty evaluation is a delicate procedure and that few are sensitive enough to differentiate between levels of performance. However, "optimum efficiency" has varying levels, assuming that 75 per cent of the faculty is performing at optimum effectiveness. What about the other 25 per cent? In an era of tight money, of increasing outside inquiries about accountability, and of student impatience with the minority of college teachers who are not "measuring up," sensitive and effective measures are needed. Colleges and universities, private

5

and public, need to take the leadership in this area before less sensitive and competent outside agencies take the responsibility into their own hands.

The question of across-the-board raises for everyone is a complex matter, bringing into play deep emotions as well as educational philosophy. For example, if a college emphasizes student-directed learning situations—opportunities for individual investigation and growth—the measurable aspects of this process are difficult. How can one measure self-esteem, self-understanding, and self-confidence, all of which are certainly vital aspects of personal development? Without arguing these attributes, one can argue their measurability. Trial-and-error is a legitimate but not the only aspect of the learning process, and other goals, such as competence in a particular subject, can be measured with some accuracy. Even courses that are student developed and taught with minimum content organization are judged good or bad by both students and teachers.

The civil service promotion is also contrary to the basic traditions of university life. Because the recognition accorded university professors has been based upon how well their activities are received, the professor is closer to the private entrepreneur than to the civil service worker. This distinction is vital. A similar point of view is expressed by the Cox Commission on the Columbia University student riots: "Any tendency to treat a university as business enterprise with faculty as employees and students as customers diminishes its vitality and communal cohesion" (1968, p. 196). And the first report of the Assembly on University Goals and Governance of the American Academy of Arts and Sciences (1971, p. 17) states: "The principle of differential rewards for merit in teaching and scholarship, which exists for very good reasons, should not be tampered with where it still prevails."

Overall evaluation inevitable. Evaluation of some sort, by someone, does take place. The question is whether the procedures used and the individuals using them constitute an optimal process. As Priest (1967, p. 287) points out, "Evaluation is an inherent element of any organized effort to achieve a goal." No one likes to be evaluated, however, and it is a threatening procedure regardless

6

of how it is approached. Most of us would prefer to rely upon our own instincts and experiences for an on-going self-evaluation. But such evaluation is limited by its nature:

> Tell me, good Brutus, can you see your face?

> No, Cassius, for the eye sees not itself
> But by reflection, by some other things. . . .

Whether the individual wishes it, evaluation does take place. This point is obvious to the young, nontenured college teachers, but how about the older professor who has tenure and detailed knowledge of the institution? How is he evaluated? The present situation calls for self-evaluation as the prime procedure. Rare is the person who just doesn't give a damn, and, even here, lack of challenge or opportunity—the circumstances—usually is more to blame than anything else. Almost everyone wants to perform better because he feels better when things are moving along and when improvement is taking place.

Every college teacher is discussed and analyzed often from midnight to 2:00 A.M. And every college teacher is scrutinized by colleagues, even if from afar and if upon nonclassroom data. Yet how many colleagues have ever asked one another for an evaluation of teaching performance?

How do professors view teaching evaluation? Gaff, Wilson, and others (1970, p. 29) reached this conclusion from their 1968 survey:

> Seventy-two per cent of the faculty said they favored a formal procedure to evaluate teaching. Eighty-two per cent of those in favor felt that students should be involved in the evaluation, 76 per cent felt that colleagues and 73 felt that departmental chairmen should also be involved. . . . In [a] 1970 survey, 85 per cent of the respondents endorsed the idea that a formal program of teacher evaluations of faculty should be "used by the college in making decisions about such matters as salary, promotion, and tenure."

Every evaluation system can be improved. Some contend that teaching is an art and far too complex ever to be reduced to a set of questions or too subtle to be observed perceptively by outsiders. Lorge notes that "all measurement ultimately has a residual of uncertainty that affects the certainty of causality" (1951, p. 553). The student gallops through a century of American history in ten or twelve weeks, and what does he gain besides course credit? Will the course help him see either man's wisdom and social concern or man's inhumanity to man? Will it help him understand his own place in history? Will it help him to develop a sense of proportion? He may read a dozen books and receive an A, but has he really grasped the purpose and intent of the subject if he does not understand the larger vistas and meanings of history? And how can all this be captured on an evaluation form, through a classroom visitation, or by some other means?

Professional improvement should be the primary objective of any faculty evaluation procedure, but one should have no illusions about perfection. McKeachie points out that "teaching is like an art in that it involves value judgments, and the means for achieving these values are complex. Research has revealed that many variables interact in determining teaching effectiveness. But it is the very complexity of the teaching situation that makes every bit of empirical information the more precious" (1967, p. 211). And from his study of faculty promotion practices in 584 colleges and universities, Gustad concludes: "A perfectly reliable and valid system of evaluation may, in fact, be for the foreseeable future unattainable; nevertheless, the history of learning, particularly of science, would seem to support the notion that given time, effort, and the kind of critical appraisal that identifies blind alleys, reasonable approximations to a goal can be obtained" (1961, p. 2).

Some academicians judge faculty evaluation in terms of absolutes. Since evaluation techniques and procedures for faculty evaluation are less than perfect, they would throw out any advancements that could be made. This is an idealistic—and unrealistic—position. Hungate refers to the subjective and human element in

8

evaluation: "There can be no rational improvement in institutional services without the exercise of value judgments concerning all aspects of operation. Indeed, every act of management reflects such judgments. The concern is to provide more adequate bases for them and hence to increase their reliability" (1964, p. 184).

Others would challenge the validity of evaluative procedures in general and student appraisal procedures in particular, asking: "How do we know that the appraisal procedure is able to identify outstanding or poor teaching?" In other words, how do we know that the professor who is highly rated by students is, in fact, an outstanding teacher? The question is a fair one in view of the inadequate research basis that has been built in this particular area, but we do have some research evidence. The Center for Research and Development in Higher Education conducted a study of university teaching for the Davis campus of the University of California which discloses three principal findings (Hildebrand and Wilson, 1970, p. 3): "(1) There is excellent agreement among students, and between faculty and students, about the effectiveness of given teachers. (2) Best and worst teachers engage in the same professional activities and allocate their time among academic pursuits in about the same ways. The mere performance of activities associated with teaching does not assure that the instruction is effective. (3) Eighty-five items are listed that characterize best teachers as perceived by students, and fifty-four items are listed that characterize best teachers as perceived by colleagues. All items statistically discriminate best from worst teachers with a high level of confidence."

The Purdue Rating Scale for Instruction was initially developed in 1926, and extensive and intensive research has accompanied its various refinements. This research, in essence, concludes: "A third of a century of use . . . by many teachers and a very considerable amount of experimental research . . . have demonstrated that student evaluation is a useful, convenient, reliable, and valid means of self-supervision and self-improvement for the teacher" (Remmers and Weisbrodt, 1965, p. 1). And from his study of the literature on the question of validity, McKeachie writes that, "in summary, student ratings do have some validity. Teachers rated as effective by students tend to be those teachers whose students learn most" (1969).

A final point is not "hard" in terms of research but attaches some validity to human judgment. Over a period of time, one develops a validity-feel for an appraisal form. If several dozen teachers who are acknowledged as outstanding by their peers receive high ratings on the appraisal form, some de facto validity may be claimed. Until further research provides firmer evidence, the judgmental element will continue to play a significant role and should not be ignored.

Professional development and evaluation. Professional development—self-renewal—should be available to every faculty member in one form or another: sabbatical and research leaves, summer grants, workshops, postdoctoral scholarships, and the like. In most cases faculty development opportunities are eagerly sought, most often by those dynamic and exemplary professors who, in a sense, need them least.

The overall academic load of the average professor is seriously misunderstood by those outside the academic community. The hours spent in the classroom need to be considered on a two-to-one basis: two hours of preparation and evaluation for every hour in the classroom. A twelve-hour classroom teaching load, considered normal for most undergraduate teaching assignments, becomes thirty-six hours of teaching and teaching-related activities. Add a conservative estimate of five hours a week for advising and counseling, five hours for committee and departmental activities, four hours for correspondence and other academic housekeeping details, and the total becomes fifty hours per week—and the professor has not even begun to do the reading, studying, and research that are essential to keep him on the growing edge of his field. This being the case, and with every field of knowledge literally bursting at the seams, it is not difficult to make the case for professional leaves and sabbaticals for all academic personnel.

On the other side of the coin, professional development should be urged for instructors who are not demonstrating success in those areas that are their primary responsibility. This practice

Basic Assumptions and Operational Procedures

reflects the positive dimension of evaluation—the effort to remedy weaknesses uncovered through evaluative procedures. The American Academy of Arts and Sciences, while defending the importance of tenure, recommends that "means ought to be developed to encourage and facilitate the early departure of those who are making small contributions to their institution and their students" (1971, p. 18). But before such steps are taken (just procedures for bringing about early departure have not as yet been developed in collegial institutions), every effort should be made to renew and energize the individual.

The traditional sabbatical leave, in fact, is no longer sufficient to cover the diverse needs and interests of faculty members. Indeed, even the derivation of the word (from *Sabbath,* which is the seventh day and a day of rest) is out of keeping with contemporary needs. Most faculty members prefer short and frequent leaves, and "rest period" hardly describes most sabbaticals. In addition to consideration of a system of leaves at the departmental level, each professor or administrator needs to consider systematic procedures for individual self-renewal, by raising such questions as: (1) Am I actively involved in some systematic professional renewal activity, such as a piece of research or a study of research and literature? (Good teaching is based upon scholarly activity and professional liveliness, and one important avenue is through research, writing, and systematic study.) (2) What kinds of faculty development would be most useful to me? (Alternatives: seminars for improved teaching, release of time, exchange of professorships, leave of absence, and sabbatical leave.) (3) What is my definition of an outstanding teacher? How well do I fit it?

What appraisal should accomplish. Gage (1959) identifies three reasons for evaluating teaching: the traditional need for providing a broad base for administrative decisions on promotions, salaries, and tenure; the new concern for evaluation as a basis for professional improvement and development; and the need for data for further research on teaching and learning. Appraisal should provide feedback and guidance as well as judgment. The positive and constructive dimensions of evaluation—feedback and guidance

—have not been given adequate consideration in most schemes of appraisal. In essence, appraisal should improve professional performance; that is its overall purpose. This goal needs to remain paramount in the minds of administrators and faculty alike.

The operational principles I now discuss move these basic assumptions a step closer to realization. These principles are guidelines for developing appraisal procedures and are the basis for the operational procedures discussed in the next two chapters.

Individualized evaluation. Individualization has become a dominant theme on all levels of American education. Gross and undifferentiated procedures for meeting individual differences are coming under increasing criticism as more is learned about complexities of human capabilities and as better techniques of measurement are developed. "Undifferentiated procedures," unfortunately, applies to many methods for faculty evaluation. Procedures to measure faculty performance should be individualized in terms of providing more than the usual three or four categories of activities (teaching, research, public and professional service) and in terms of adjusting categories, as much as circumstances permit, to the interests of the individual.

The traditional stereotype of the professor as an absent-minded, kindly, detached, and elderly gentleman no longer fits the world of the "action intellectual" about whom Theodore A. White has written—a man who moves with authority and relevance in and out of business, government, and education. If an agricultural bias was evident in public universities and colleges during the past half century, an urban bias may be dominant for at least the remainder of this century. Evaluation of faculty performance becomes more difficult in the urban environment because of the more diverse nature of the student body and the greater diversity in professional activities. In view of many changes and increasing complexities, an individually developed evaluative grid—in line with the objectives of the institution and the department—provides optimum flexibility and individualization. The grid should consider three dimensions: the nature of the institution, the nature of the department, and individual interests and abilities.

Few institutions of higher education have developed long-range and short-range objectives for the academic program. Unless the setting of goals is taken seriously and unless some hard decisions are made about which goals are most important, a system of faculty evaluation cannot be tied effectively to institutional goals.

Determination of academic objectives should reckon with some desired balance among the nine criteria discussed in the next chapter on operational procedures. If an institution has national prestige as a major goal, then professional status may receive weight; if the focus is on teaching, then classroom performance and advising may receive major attention; and so on.

A systematic and comprehensive plan for improving overall academic performance through appraisal of faculty performance does require an active role for the department chairman and the dean. It is at the departmental level that the major sifting of information and evidence about each faculty member can best take place, and should. Decentralization of managerial responsibilities from the dean to the department chairman is a national trend caused by the increasing bureaucratic functions that threaten to inundate the dean's office, by the increasing specialization of subject content that puts competence to appraise scholarly performance below the dean's level, and by the sheer increase in numbers of faculty members. It is interesting to note the increase in the number of periodical articles and convention programs that focus on the role and function of the department chairman. (For a detailed discussion of the role of the department chairman, see Dressel, Johnson, and Marcus, 1970.)

Within the mission of the institution and within that developed for the division or college, there is flexibility as to the departmental thrust(s). Will a political science department, for example, decide to focus on the city, state, or federal levels? Will it decide to focus on young teachers who are interested in developing mathematical models for decision making or will it seek others who have broad experiences? These questions need some clarification before a plan for overall faculty performance can have optimum benefit.

Individual interests and strengths should rule the day within the purposes and directions of the institution, the division or college, and the department. Late in the spring term, the department chairman should confer with each faculty member about what professional courses and activities he prefers for the next academic year and summer. Securing all desired courses and activities may not be possible for any one professor in view of such considerations as basic departmental offerings and other factors, but the matter should be explored. One faculty member might want to develop a new course and therefore be relieved of one course for a semester; another might be relieved of two courses in order to finish a book; and yet another individual might teach a course in another discipline.

The conference also should result in agreement on weighing the criteria for evaluation of the individual's overall performance. For example, one faculty member might have 50 per cent of his performance based upon teaching and the other 50 per cent upon other criteria; another might have 85 per cent based upon classroom teaching; and still another might have 75 per cent based upon special reports. These determinations need always to consider institution, college, and department needs, but it simply does not make sense—indeed, it is antirational—to expect all faculty members to follow some predetermined formula that treats everyone alike.

Sources of input. The total array of professional activities, with teaching foremost, is too diverse and complex to be fairly evaluated by one input. However, one systematic and reliable procedure is better than any number of casual and highly subjective ones. The in thing at the time of this writing is student evaluation of faculty teaching. Some officials and professors have just discovered this dimension of evaluation, although at least one institution of higher education has used the procedure for forty years and others have a decade or more of experience with it. Yet student evaluation of teaching has not been used extensively according to Gustad (1967, p. 270), who found a "substantial decline in the use of systematic student ratings between 1961 and 1966." His evidence was gathered as part of two studies sponsored by the American Council on Education. The results of his research are given in Table 1. I speculate that the decline found by Gustad relates to the rapid growth in colleges and universities during this period, which brought to the foreground problems of coping with larger numbers and new programs.

No evidence is available for the five-year period between 1966 and 1971, but a significant increase in systematic student evaluation of teaching has taken place. One reactor to Gustad's report—James A. Johnson, a student with close connections to the National Student Association—points out that he has observed an increase in systematic student evaluation (1967, p. 290); and Gaff and Wilson note that in 1971, of the "feasible procedures which have been used to obtain systematic evidence about teaching, . . . by far the most prevalent is [student ratings]" (1971).

Management and utilization of evaluative data. Too many procedures for evaluation consider only the first step, the development of evaluative criteria. Although this initial step is important, effective and sensitive procedures for evaluation can fail unless sufficient attention is given two other processes: procedures for evaluation and their application, and the final weighing. Most failures of evaluation schemes are publicly attributed to faulty content when, in fact, the culprit is likely to be faulty management and utilization of data.

The comprehensive approach to faulty evaluation which I recommend makes four assumptions: those using the evaluation criteria have some objectives or goals in mind; the system will be used positively; the system is manageable in terms of time required for processing; and the system is economical in terms of time spent and results achieved. Most systems of student evaluation should be computerized, using optical scanning devices if available. Appendix A outlines the North Carolina State computer experience with student evaluations.

Strategies for implementation. Obviously no one strategy for implementation works in all instances, or even in most, but the

Table 1. Comparisons by Rank Orders of Sources of Information Employed in the Evaluation of Teaching

Source	Universities[a] 1961 (N = 130)	Universities[a] 1966 (N = 110)	Liberal Arts Colleges 1961 (N = 272)	Liberal Arts Colleges 1966 (N = 484)	Teachers Colleges 1961 (N = 29)	Teachers Colleges 1966 (N = 133)	Junior Colleges 1961 (N = 25)	Junior Colleges 1966 (N = 128)
Chairman evaluation	1	1	2[b]	2	1	1	6[b]	2
Dean evaluation	6	2	4	1	3	2	—	1
Scholarly research and publication	—	3	—	5	—	4	—	15
Colleagues' opinions	4[b]	4	5[b]	3	5	3	4[b]	7
Informal student opinions	2	5	1	4	4	6	2	5
Committee evaluations	11[b]	6	15[b]	8	—	9	—	12
Grade distributions	11[b]	7	11[b]	6	—	7	4[b]	6
Student examination performance	7	8	7[b]	9	12	10	10[b]	9
Enrollment in elective courses	13	9	10	11	—	13	9	14
Systematic student ratings	4[b]	10	5[b]	12[b]	6	15	6[b]	11
Self-evaluation	15[b]	11	11[b]	10	—	11	—	10
Course syllabi and examinations	9	12	11[b]	7	9[b]	5	3	4
Alumni opinions	14	13	7[b]	12[b]	9[b]	12	—	13
Classroom visits	3	14	2[b]	15	2	8	1	3
Long-term follow-up of students	10	15	9	14	—	14	8	8
Informal methods	8	—	11[b]	—	7	—	—	—
Student behavior	15[b]	—	15[b]	—	8	—	—	—
Other	15[b]	—	17	—	9[b]	—	10[b]	—

[a] College of arts and sciences only.
[b] Rank shared with another source.
Source: Gustad, 1967.

following guidelines may be helpful. (For another strategy, see Eble, 1970.)

First, both the president and the chief academic officer of the college must support and be knowledgeable about the plan, which may or may not be administratively initiated, depending on institutional patterns. Administrative support is necessary to break log jams as well as to give the plan campuswide scope. In large universities, strong pressures may be brought to bear by those advocating different procedures for different colleges within the university. Administrators and those in charge of the study need to hold the line against this dilution if the desire is to view the institution as a whole; yet a section in the overall procedure can be developed, or another section added, to meet the special needs of a particular college. (Required vs voluntary evaluation is discussed further in the last chapter.)

Second, nothing replaces the hard work necessary to develop an evaluation program, and this work may include special studies— statistical and computer analyses and anecdotal reports. Any report that is hastily prepared or is full of intellectual gaps has only a minimal chance of success. It is better not to undertake implementation of an overall system of faculty evaluation unless adequate time and enthusiasm are available to see the task through.

Third, trial runs improve the instrument as well as reduce the anxiety level. In many colleges and universities, professors with ten to fifteen years of tenured service have been evaluated long ago or never. To them, the system represents a threat—the degree of which may be inversely proportional to their knowledge about it (depending, of course, upon the quality of the system). As they become knowledgeable about the instrument and aware of its positive features, their anxiety level probably will decrease. The reaction of senior professors toward the system significantly influences its chances of success.

Fourth, faculty resistance points shall be anticipated and dealt with positively. Megaw describes the "ignoble" factors of fear and laziness: "The nightmarish fear of being declared incompetent or at least shamefully inexpert affects only the less able teacher, but

17

a lighter version, a competitive nervousness about one's ranking in relation to one's rivals, may extend to the highest level of faculty ability." And with respect to laziness, he refers not to "a general, undifferentiated laziness, . . .—most teachers put in a long working day—but a special laziness of the experimental spirit: reluctance, in short, to consider new patterns of overwork." Several professionally valid reasons need to be faced realistically. One is the view that "what goes on in the classroom is vastly more complex than any definition of it and that its chief values reside in this complexity" (1967, pp. 282–283).

Misuse of results is another common concern among faculty members, and in some cases the fear is well founded. It is a serious mistake for administrators to use only faculty evaluation as a means for making decisions on promotion, tenure, and salary increases. While all evidence should be consulted in making such decisions, the primary focus of faculty evaluation should be positive—upon improvement of teaching and learning.

Some institutions are using poor evaluative instruments and procedures; the faculty and the administration know it, but no action is taken to remedy the situation. About the only positive thing that can be said about such a circumstance is that it affects everyone equally. These situations, however, do create poor morale and a negative attitude toward evaluation in general.

Fifth, faculty forums or open hearings are desirable, and at a point when the document is open to modification. A mailing of the procedure should precede the forum so some basic knowledge about the plan can be acquired. But do not assume that it has. Each forum should review carefully the need for, and nature of, the procedure. Those explaining the procedure should be chosen for their coolness under cross-examination, acceptance by the faculty, and knowledge and support of the procedure. (Some nontenured faculty members should be included.) The official student channels and the student newspaper should have access to the forums, and the newspaper should be encouraged to give good coverage to the procedure. The entire procedure may succeed or fail on the basis of these informal forums, which points up the importance of planning carefully for them.

Sixth, provide ample time for the overall process of implementation. "Ample" time is an institutional matter and may vary from one term to two years. The teaching faculty and administration need to feel somewhat comfortable with the procedure and to believe it is reasonably fair. "Somewhat" and "reasonably" may seem less than ideal, and they are, but when one considers the fact that no one particularly enjoys being evaluated, especially in a detailed and systematic manner, the allowance of ample time may permit the procedure to endure.

One might ask at this point: "Isn't the overall procedure of implementation outlined here an avoidance of the inevitable problems the new procedure will bring with it? Isn't initiation by administrative action more realistic?" This procedure may be effective in some institutions, but generally speaking it is not, for one basic reason: Curricular and instructional programs in most colleges or universities are initiated by faculty members. They have tenure, have the intricate infrastructural knowledge, and usually see presidents and deans come and go. If a system is repugnant to large numbers of faculty members, they can find various ways of noncompliant "compliance" that seriously compromises the effectiveness of the procedure.

The extent of initial opposition should not be determined by a vote. A vote early may serve to polarize positions and decrease effective dialogue. If the storm signals are up, those developing the procedure should analyze four possible trouble spots: the evaluative instruments, the introductory process, the readiness of the faculty, and the timing. Rather than putting the procedure into action over strong opposition, the developers may want to take one step backward before moving ahead again. A core of strong opposition to the overall procedure can be expected in any case. How large is this core and whom does it involve? One needs to be careful about overreacting to the opposition for fear of driving some moderates into the opposition corner. The opposition should be given every

19

opportunity to make their case either in writing or in an open forum. These methods can challenge the developers of the overall procedure to secure ample evidence and to sharpen their arguments.

The follow-up appraisal of the procedure itself may be either a sophisticated one with samplings of student and faculty reactions through a carefully conducted survey and interview technique or a more informal method. But plans for the follow-up evaluation should be spelled out in the initial presentation of the procedure, as an example of following recommended professional practice which calls for an internal evaluative method as an assist to the credibility of the procedure.

In essence, strategies for implementation need time, careful planning, openness, administrative support, and probably a bit of luck. The content needs to be good and adequate research should be evident on what is being proposed.

Chapter 2

The Professor as Teacher

*A*ctivities considered relevant to evaluation are most often confined to research, teaching, service, and professional activities. These activities are basic to any scheme for evaluation, but in discussing the category problem with many educators, a general uneasiness was found with respect to the limitations of using just four categories. College teachers today are engaging in a much wider range of activities than in the past, and this expansion should be reflected in a greater range of categories. To this end, the following nine categories are suggested: classroom teaching, advising, faculty service and relations, management (administration), performing and visual arts, professional services, publications, public service, and research.

The reinstatement of classroom teaching as the raison d'etre for undergraduate education has become quite evident on the college and university scene, largely due to student discontent, to financial exigencies, and to re-examination of goals and philosophy. Although the small private and public colleges traditionally have emphasized classroom teaching, the majority of undergraduate stu-

21

dents have been enrolled in medium to large universities where graduate study and research have received much attention.

John Gardner's call for greater emphasis on undergraduate teaching—"First, we must restore the status of teaching" (1968, p. 1)—is echoed by the American Academy of Arts and Sciences: "Like other complex institutions, colleges and universities have varied purposes. Foremost among them must be learning. . . . Research—important as it is—and public service are appropriate to colleges and universities when they contribute to learning, its advancement as well as its transmission and utilization, and are consonant with those academic freedoms on which learning depends. To say that the theses emphasize learning as the goal to which governance should be directed is not to be nostalgic or romantic about the past but to assert a purpose that has not been sufficiently central in the past or in the present" (1971, pp. 6–7).

Sometimes those who are closest to the scene, professors and administrators, lose sight of the overall impact of their classroom labors. Sanford reminds us of this point when he writes (1967, pp. 166–167):

> One way to understand the importance of college teaching is to ask some recent graduates, "What was the most significant thing that happened to you in college?" The chances are good that in one way or another their key experience involved a teacher. When I put this question to a young alumna of one of our women's colleges, she recalled two experiences that were very important to her. The first was a freshman seminar in which the teacher made her feel that what she had to say was being listened to and was a worthwhile contribution to the group. It was here that she first learned to value the use of the mind; she developed a commitment to her education and became an "A" student. The second experience occurred in her senior year. A professor had assigned a difficult paper, which she completed and turned in, fully expecting her usual 'A'. But the paper was returned with a grade of 'D'. When she inquired the reason, the professor spent a long time pointing out the weaknesses of the work—'about an hour on the first page, another on the second, and so on.' By page three this young woman had learned a great deal about humility,

about what it takes to do good work, and about what a teacher can do for a student.

There is general agreement upon the necessity for the reinstatement of classroom teaching to center stage, but as for the procedures used to evaluate this teaching, there remain many variations and conflicts. Table 2 lists the frequency with which various evaluative sources were used in 1100 colleges and universities.

Table 2. FREQUENCY OF USE OF VARIOUS SOURCES OF INFORMATION IN THE EVALUATION OF TEACHING EFFECTIVENESS

Source of Information	Used in All or Most Departments (%)	Not Used (%)
Chairman evaluation	85.1	3.4
Dean evaluation	82.3	5.8
Colleagues' opinions	48.9	8.7
Scholarly research and publications	43.8	21.6
Informal student opinions	41.2	9.6
Grade distributions	28.0	37.4
Course syllabi and examinations	26.4	28.0
Committee evaluation	25.1	52.4
Student examination performance	19.6	35.8
Self-evaluation or report	16.3	57.2
Classroom visits	14.0	39.5
Systematic student ratings	12.4	47.6
Enrollment in elective courses	11.0	49.9
Long-term follow-up of students	10.2	47.1
Alumni opinions	9.9	46.8

Source: Austin and Lee, 1967.

Much has happened since the spring of 1966, when the Austin and Lee study was completed, the most dramatic change being the significantly increased use of student evaluations. But in spite of this increase, one has to agree with this observation by Austin and Lee (1967, p. 299): "If the ultimate measure of the teacher's effectiveness is his impact on the student—a view which few educators would dispute—it is unfortunate that those sources of information most likely to yield information about this influence are least likely to be used."

GOOD TEACHING

In his extensive research on teacher effectiveness, Ryans finds three prominent patterns of observable classroom behavior or behaving styles: "Pattern X—friendly, understanding, sympathetic teacher behavior; Pattern Y—responsible, businesslike, systematic teacher behavior; and Pattern Z—stimulating, imaginative teacher behavior" (1967, p. 59). Mitzel adds, however, that "more than a half-century of research effort has not yielded meaningful, measurable criteria around which the majority of the nation's educators can rally. No standards exist which are commonly agreed upon as *the* criteria of teacher effectiveness" (1960, p. 148).

A general picture of good teaching can be developed, and what emerges is not particularly different from that employed by Socrates and by Plato—both quite different teachers. In a 1969 study, completed by the Center for Research and Development in Higher Education at Berkeley, Eble cites a selected sampling of student opinion at the University of California, Davis campus (1970, pp. 99–100). From an extensive list of teacher traits, these eight emerged as most important: is a dynamic and energetic person (.80); explains clearly (.78); has an interesting style of presentation (.76); seems to enjoy teaching (.74); has a genuine interest in students (.74); is friendly toward students (.71); encourages class discussion (.70); discusses points of view other than his own (.70).

Another study, centering on criteria for effective teaching, was completed by the University of Toledo's Office of Institutional Research (1969). Thirteen thousand six hundred and forty-three responses from students, faculty, and alumni were read and categorized into sixty effective teaching behaviors. These behaviors were then rated as to importance by 1793 students, faculty, and alumni. (See Table 3 for twelve highest ratings and value factors.)

Good teaching can be identified from various research

Table 3. RATINGS AND VALUE FACTORS

	Stu-dents	Alum-ni	Fac-ulty	All	Value Factor
Being well prepared for class	1	1	1	1	.78
Establishing sincere interest in subject being taught	2	2	6	2	.74
Demonstrating comprehensive knowledge of his subject	4	6	2	3	.73
Using teaching methods which enable students to achieve objectives of the course	5	3	10	4	.73
Constructing tests which search for understanding on part of students rather than rote memory ability	7	4	8	5	.73
Being fair and reasonable to students in evaluation procedures	3	9	5	6	.73
Communicating effectively at levels appropriate to the preparedness of students	6	7	8	7	.73
Encouraging intelligent independent thought by students	11	5	3	8	.73
Organizing the course in logical fashion	8	10	11	9	.72
Motivating students to do their best	12	8	4	10	.71
Treating students with respect	10	11	9	11	.71
Acknowledging all questions to the best of his ability	9	14	12	12	.70

Source: R. R. Perry, 1969.

25

procedures, as indicated by the two studies that are cited. While no single list of traits can be developed, some qualities stand out—those having to do with professional competence, personal interest in students, fairness, and positive attitude.

Five procedures for evaluating classroom teaching are given in this chapter: student evaluation, classroom visitation, teaching materials and procedures, special incident, and self-evaluation. The specific weighing of all or some of these components should be determined by each individual, department, and/or institution.

STUDENT EVALUATION

Teachers need to listen to students to find out whether or not they are learning and, if so, what. As Johnson points out:

> It is often the individual student who knows best whether or not he is learning. It is the student who knows best when he cannot understand or already knows what is being discussed. It is the student who knows a course is stimulating him to learn more about a subject or whether it is boring him to death. It is the student who can best formulate those fundamental and personal questions so bothering him that he cannot proceed to other academic matters. It is the student who can best evaluate when he is beginning to integrate the process of learning with the problems he continually confronts in life (1967, pp. 289–90).

Student evaluation should utilize a carefully designed and tested instrument, and judgment needs to be exercised in its usage. For example, teaching evaluations of the first-year college teacher should serve primarily as a diagnostic procedure for improving classroom teaching. One also needs to consider whether a professor is teaching in an area outside his major strength. This sometimes is necessary to fill unexpected gaps in departmental offerings, but it will often affect the ratings.

The student teaching-appraisal form on page 28 is based upon a definition of good teaching drawn from a composite of the literature and from professional colleagues, and modified by students. It is this: A good teacher personifies enthusiasm for his students, the area of competence, and life itself. He knows his subject,

26

can explain it clearly, and is willing to do so—in or out of class. Class periods are interesting, and at times, alive with excitement. He approaches his area of competence and his students with integrity that is neither stiff nor pompous, and his attitude and demeanor are more caught than taught.

Student-initiated evaluation of classroom teaching has mushroomed in the past two or three years, and some excellent and sensitive programs have been developed. Others, however, leave much to be desired in terms of both motivation and operation. If the motive is to find evidence to support the conclusion that the campus abounds with poor teaching, then the objectivity, acceptance, and effectiveness of the instrument will suffer. The operation will suffer, too, if it is not carefully planned and if adequate funds are not available. Also, provisions need to be made for quality controls as student governments change and the initiators of the program graduate. Students also should be aware of the legal implications of their findings. The instrument, the sampling, and the procedure need to be carefully planned and carried out so that a professor does not receive an unjust rating.

The most effective way for a college or university to cope with student-initiated evaluation is for the faculty and administration to develop a sound and sensitive procedure for student evaluation of teaching. As Howe points out, "We have the obvious fact that students do pay for the instruction they receive; they are not simply a necessary evil to be tolerated as part of the educational endeavor, but are the purpose of it. The opinions of those who eat the pudding certainly ought to be considered if we wish to know how the pudding tastes" (1967, p. 260).

In the application of the student evaluation procedure, the instrument should be used twice per school term rather than once. Given early in the term, the evaluation is used only by the teacher, who compares student responses with his personal rating on the self-evaluation form (page 37). This early-term evaluation allows the teacher some appraisal of his classroom performance at a point when time is left for modification. Research at Baldwin-Wallace on the student appraisal form included administering it early in the

STUDENT APPRAISAL OF TEACHING

Teacher .... Course ....

Term .... Academic Year ....

Thoughtful student reaction can help improve teaching effectiveness. This questionnaire is designed for that purpose. Your assistance is appreciated. Please do not sign your name.

At the option of the instructor, questions 15 and 16 may be added. Use the back of this form for any further comments you might want to express.

Directions:

Rate your teacher on each item, giving the highest scores for unusually effective performances. Place in the blank space before each statement the number that most nearly expresses your view:

Highest			Average			Lowest	Don't Know
7	6	5	4	3	2	1	X

.... 1. Have the major objectives of the course been made clear?

.... 2. How do you rate agreement between course objectives and lesson assignments?

.... 3. How well are class presentations planned and organized?

.... 4. Are important ideas clearly explained?

.... 5. How would you judge the professor's mastery of the course content?

.... 6. Is class time well used?

.... 7. Does the professor encourage critical thinking and analysis?

.... 8. Does your professor encourage you to seek his help when necessary?

.... 9. Does the professor encourage relevant student involvement in the class?

.... 10. How does the professor react to student viewpoints different from his own?

.... 11. How would you describe the attitude of fellow class members toward your professor?

.... 12. Are you being graded fairly in this class?

.... 13. Considering the previous 12 items, how would you rate this teacher in comparison to all others you have had in the department?

.... 14. In comparison to all others you have had in the institution as a whole?

.... 15.

.... 16.

.... Composite rating.

term and again near the end of the course. The product moment correlation of the two tests was .68, with significance at the .01 level of confidence. A higher correlation between early and late administrations of the test would indicate little improvement between the early and late testing, which would not be as desirable as a somewhat lower correlation, with improvement at the end of the course. See Appendix B for a report on this research.

Several procedures for distributing and collecting the data can be developed, and one should be aware of the sensitivities that may be related to both aspects. Eble has suggested that the distribution and collection processes should consider three criteria: objectivity, coverage, and timing. About objectivity, he writes: "In the actual administration of the questionnaires, some distance should be preserved between the faculty member whose course or courses are being evaluated and the students doing the evaluating. Filling out the questionnaires under the eyes of the faculty member who has handed them out and plans to take them up, though it may testify to a highly desirable degree of trust between the faculty member and student, may also inhibit or distort the response" (1970, p. 24). In relation to this, a research study at the University of Kentucky, reported by Kirchner, investigated student ratings when the instructor was present as compared with those when he was absent. Student ratings were statistically higher—significantly so—when the instructor was in the room (1969). It is important that this procedure be standardized for greater reliability. Likewise, some objective and standardized procedure for distributing, collecting, and delivering the questionnaires should be developed. Professors may be insensitive to the reluctance of students to be completely honest if they have the slightest suspicion that the professor will see their replies. Most students, for example, believe that the professor can recognize their handwriting.

The extent of campus coverage depends upon what is sought from the evaluation. A campus-wide approach, for example, allows comparisons between and among various disciplines. In any case, the instrument needs the flexibility that will allow it to serve fairly diverse disciplines. (The final blank questions in the example given allow some latitude, or other individualized sections might be developed.)

If the questionnaire is carried out of class by students and returned later or deposited at a designated point, the percent of return may be a factor. Eble (1970, p. 25) cites the carefully administered Princeton surveys, which were university-wide and returned by the students. The return rate was 95 per cent for the first term, 78 per cent for the second term, and 76 per cent the following term. If the percentage of returns for any one class is below 70, the results may be of questionable validity.

Cost enters into the application of the procedure, and some colleges on the quarter system therefore use the instrument for only two out of the three quarters.

Some colleges and universities include the appraisal ratings in the individual's personnel folder while others maintain separate appraisal files. This matter likely will be determined by the size of the institution as well as the propinquity between the personnel folders and the processing center for the appraisal forms.

Care must be taken that the evaluative instrument does not acquire a punitive connotation. Student appraisal of teaching should have as its primary purpose the improvement of teaching performance although the results also should enter into judgments about merit increases, promotions, tenure, and institutional severance. It would be wrong not to use every piece of valid evidence to reach the fairest possible decision about personnel evaluation, but the improvement of teaching should be the primary purpose of student evaluation.

CLASSROOM VISITATION

Classroom visitation may be an aspect of teaching evaluation, depending upon the institutional pattern. Such visitations should be planned with care and the results need to be interpreted methodically. Some professors may object to observation, however, and on this matter, Silber, president of Boston University, commented: "I have heard professors argue that this [classroom observation] violates the dignity of the profession. I heard a very good response to that by a professor of English at Virginia, who said: 'What a curious concept of dignity that a man should be ashamed to be caught at his work," (1968). Hodgkinson (n.d.) describes the classroom visitation experience at Bard College where he served as dean:

> In this plan, every junior faculty member who is eligible for tenure or for promotion is visited by several senior members of his department or division over a period of time. The senior member must consult the junior member before the class, finding out what is to be attempted and what the previous history of the class has been. He must then stay for the full length of the period, have a conference with the instructor after the class is over, and write a fairly extensive comment on what he has seen. A copy of this comment goes to the instructor and a copy goes to the department or divisional chairman. The reason for this is simply to make sure that everyone understands the senior member's judgment, and he then feels committed to say the same thing to his senior colleagues that he said in the letter to the junior member. These evaluations are often longitudinal in nature in that they talk about the person's previous performance, where he now is, where he seems to go, and they usually mention some specific ways in which the person can be helped to get there. Thus they serve not only the purpose of being a decision-making device but also of providing a teacher with some specific ways in which he may improve, for use throughout the year. It is also possible for junior members to visit the classes of senior members to see them exemplify the comments that they make in their comments to the junior members. This has a salutory effect on the senior member's evaluations. This approach, of course, is subject to human frailty. What approach is not? However it provides for richness of interpretation which the typical monolithic standardized student test score does not.

Care must be taken that the observer does not screen the teacher's performance too much through his own selective perceptions of what constitutes good teaching. Not one but three prominent patterns of observable classroom teaching styles were mentioned

31

earlier, and each one can be excellent. (For additional information on classroom visitation see Medley and Mitzel, 1963; Gray, 1969; and Eastman, 1969.)

In using classroom visitation for evaluation, a modified version of the instrument for student appraisal of teaching is suggested for those making the visit (see page 33). Most of the questions remain appropriate, and the instrument can provide a useful comparison between classroom visitation and student ratings. Who should visit, how often, and for what purpose are questions that require consideration. A conference between the classroom visitor(s) and the instructor should take place within a few days following the visitation, and an analysis and interpretation of the visitation as well as the conference should be passed on to the department head, and then into the individual's personnel file.

TEACHING MATERIALS AND PROCEDURES

This category includes materials that the instructor distributes to the class: course outlines, reading assignments, and examinations. The quality of student papers written for the course also may be examined. Some colleges and universities require for every course an outline, which is available in the library for student inspection. This procedure can be helpful in student selection of courses. Although this category generally is not included in teaching appraisals, at least not in any formal manner, it can be significant and should be considered. The department chairman and/or a committee of colleagues would seem to be the logical choices as judges of materials and procedures. (See page 34 for the teaching materials appraisal form.)

SPECIAL INCIDENTS

Special incident data refers to either laudatory or negative comments about an individual's teaching. By considering special incident data as a separate category, recognition is taken of the fact that such evaluation *does* take place. Special incident includes evidences of teaching effectiveness, such as unusually fine course syllabi or course papers, or noticeable success of students in a competition that relates directly to the course. It also includes negative

CLASSROOM VISITATION APPRAISAL

Teacher .... Course ....

Term .... Academic Year ....

Visitor(s) .... Title ....

The following appraisal form contains 12 questions, many of which are found on the student appraisal of teaching form. In addition, you may want to develop a narrative description of your visitation.

Directions:

Rate teaching on each item, giving the highest scores for unusually effective performances.

Highest			Average			Lowest	Don't Know
7	6	5	4	3	2	1	X

.... 1. Were the major objectives of the course made clear to you?

.... 2. How well was the class presentation planned and organized?

.... 3. Were important ideas clearly explained?

.... 4. How would you judge the professor's mastery of the course content?

.... 5. Was class time well used?

.... 6. Did the professor encourage critical thinking and analysis?

.... 7. Do you believe the professor encouraged relevant student involvement in the class?

.... 8. How did the professor react to student viewpoints different from his own?

.... 9. How would you describe the attitude of students in the class toward the professor?

.... 10. Do you believe that your visitation was at a time when you were able to fairly judge the nature and tenor of the teaching-learning process?

.... 11. Considering the previous 10 items, how would you rate this teacher in comparison to others in the department?

.... 12. As compared with others in the institution?

.... 13.

.... 14.

.... Composite rating.

Yes .... No .... Did you have a preliminary conference with the teacher before the visitation?

Yes .... No .... Did you have a follow-up conference?

Comments after class visitation: ....

....

Comments after follow-up conference: ....

....

33

TEACHING MATERIALS AND PROCEDURES APPRAISAL

Teacher .... Course ....

Term .... Academic Year ....

Appraiser(s) .... Title of appraiser(s) ....

....

The following appraisal form contains questions which should be helpful in judging this category. Additional questions may be added. Also, you may want to add a summary statement in your own words.

Directions:

Rate each item, giving the highest scores to unusually effective teaching materials and procedures.

							Not Appro-
Highest			Average			Lowest	priate
7	6	5	4	3	2	1	X

.... 1. How would you rate the overall quality of the course outline, if one is used?

.... 2. From what the instructor distributes, or from what is said, do you believe that the students gain a coherent picture of the course?

.... 3. Do the grading procedures seem reasonable and fair?

.... 4. Do the materials reflect the most acceptable authority sources as well as new views and evidence in the field?

.... 5. From what can be gleaned from the course materials and procedures, do you believe that the students have a challenging and meaningful experience in the classroom?

.... 6. Based upon an examination of course materials and procedures, how would you rate the course preparation and teaching concern of this individual as compared with other teachers in the department?

.... 7. As compared with others in the institution as a whole?

.... 8.

.... 9.

.... Composite rating.

34

data. The special incident category allows evaluation to include the evidences of good or bad teaching that cannot be determined from the student appraisal procedure or from classroom visitation.

Care must be taken that "normal" special incident data do not assume undue importance in the evaluation of teaching. It is unfortunate that some administrators equate good teaching with the absence of criticsm. This criterion is a curious one, and it is probably more widespread than is generally believed to be the case. Such misuse of special incident data should be carefully avoided. The form on page 36 is suggested for appraising the special incident category.

SELF-EVALUATION

Although private self-evaluation is more or less continuous, even if haphazard, systematic and planned self-evaluation is rare. Formalized, conscious procedures for improving and refining self-perception are seldom developed and the majority of us need assistance in using self-evaluation deliberately and constructively. Some contend that teacher self-evaluation is a waste of time—an excessive introspection when the emphasis should be external, on the student. Furthermore, they contend that any use of such ratings in performance evaluation will skew the results upward. (For the results of a research study on teacher self-evaluation, see Simpson, 1960.)

The validity of these points cannot be refuted by evidence. There is none. Self-evaluation, however, can fall back upon considerable research on sensitivity and human awareness. We need to try new procedures and to develop research in order to understand better the positive uses of self-evaluation in performance improvement. As one develops greater self-awareness, he is able to respond more effectively to the needs and interests of others, and he is more likely to observe unspoken clues to behaviors and needs.

Two uses of self-evaluation are recommended. One is the early-term evaluation which is for the teacher's eyes only—to assist him in improving the course for the remainder of the term. The student appraisal form can be used in comparison with the teacher's self-evaluation. The second use provides the teacher with a basis for

SPECIAL INCIDENT APPRAISAL

Date ....

Appraiser .... Title ....

Highest			Average			Lowest	Don't Know
7	6	5	4	3	2	1	X

Description of incident: ....

....

....

....

....

....

....

SELF-APPRAISAL OF TEACHING

Teacher .... Course ....

Term .... Academic Year ....

Thoughtful self-evaluation can help improve teaching effectiveness. This questionnaire is designed for that purpose. You are asked to look at your own performance in teaching.

At your option, questions 12 and 13 may be added. Use the back of this form for any written comments you might want to express. These might record any unusual circumstances that relate to the course and to your teaching it.

Directions:

Rate yourself on each item, giving the highest scores for unusually effective performances. Place in the blank space before each statement the number that most nearly expresses your view:

Highest			Average			Lowest	Don't Know
7	6	5	4	3	2	1	X

.... 1. Have the major objectives of your course been made clear?

.... 2. How do you rate agreement between course objectives and lesson assignments?

.... 3. Are class presentations well planned and organized?

.... 4. Are important ideas clearly explained?

.... 5. How would you judge your mastery of the course content?

.... 6. Is class time well used?

.... 7. Have you encouraged critical thinking and analysis?

.... 8. Have you encouraged students to seek your help when necessary?

.... 9. Have you encouraged relevant student involvement in the class?

.... 10. How tolerant are you of student viewpoints that differ from your own?

.... 11. Considering the previous 10 items, how would you rate your performance in this course as compared to others in the department who have taught the same course?

.... 12.

.... 13.

.... Composite rating.

37

comparing his perceptions with those of others. This evaluation can also serve as a basis for the annual conference on academic performance between the professor and the department head and may become a percentage factor in computing overall teaching performance. Because the instrument for self-evaluation (see page 37) is quite similar to the student and visitation appraisal forms, there is a basis for comparison among three procedures.

COMPOSITE RATING

Three hypothetical cases are used to illustrate the almost endless flexibility that is possible with the system. Professor A is evaluated in this manner:

Possible Categories	Weight		Criterion Rating		Raw Score
student appraisal	50%	×	6.1	=	305
classroom visitation	10	×	5.5	=	55
teaching materials, etc.	20	×	6.2	=	124
special incident	10	×	5.9	=	59
self-evaluation	10	×	5.9	=	59
	100%				602

602 ÷ 700 = .86, which is the overall rating on classroom teaching.

The "weight" (always adding up to 100 percent) is determined by the department chairman in consultation with the faculty member. The "criterion rating" is determined by dividing the total rating score by the number of items rated. For example, if, on the student appraisal instrument, the gross score is 79 for the 13 items, then 79 divided by 13 comes to 6.1, which is the criterion rating used in computing the composite score for classroom teaching. "Raw score" is determined by multiplying weight given to the category by criterion rating. "Composite score" on classroom teaching is determined by dividing the total raw score by the total score possible, which is always 700.

Professor B is evaluated by the same criteria weighted differently:

The Professor as Teacher

Possible Categories	Weight		Criterion Rating		Raw Score
student appraisal	20%	×	6.5	=	130
classroom visitation	20	×	6.1	=	122
teaching materials, etc.	20	×	5.8	=	116
special incident	20	×	5.7	=	114
self-evaluation	20	×	6.2	=	124
					606

606 ÷ 700 = .87, which is the overall rating on classroom teaching.

Professor C presents another pattern:

Possible Categories	Weight		Criterion Rating		Raw Score
student appraisal	0%				
classroom visitation	50	×	6.2	=	310
teaching materials, etc.	25	×	6.2	=	155
special incident	10	×	5.9	=	59
self-evaluation	15	×	6.1	=	92
					616

616 ÷ 700 = .88, the overall rating for classroom teaching.

Chapter 3 ෙ෮෧෮෧෮෧෮෧෮෧෮෧෮෧

More Than a Teacher

෮෧෮෧෮෧෮෧෮෧෮෧෮෧෮෧

*W*hile classroom teaching is given greater prominence here because of its overall academic position, no attempt is made to rate the nine categories as to importance in any specific institutional setting. The direction and nature of the institution should determine these priorities. If a university decides to develop a major thrust in urban action programs, the public service and professional activities should have greater weight. If an institution decides to give greater attention to developing institutional loyalty, faculty service and relations should receive greater emphasis. Viewed in this fashion, the evaluative procedure becomes an important factor in the process of change. An institution can fashion its future significantly according to which of the activities it chooses to emphasize and to reward above others.

Neither will all nine activities apply to any one individual. The category for "performing and visual arts," for example, refers to a creative effort such as a piece of sculpture, a musical performance or composition, or a work of theatre art. Individualization of professional load is the important point.

More Than a Teacher

Related to the contemporary surge of concern about better teaching is greater attention to advising students. The problem, particularly acute with respect to the larger institutions, has arisen largely because few, if any, "brownie points" are given to professors for taking the time necessary for constructive, informed advising. Commenting upon its problems, Dressel (n.d., p. 12) has written that academic advising suffers at the undergraduate level "because few of our faculty in the present day have any conception of what undergraduate education is all about. The horizon of each professor is limited by the barriers thrust up around the disciplines and the large number of courses piled helter skelter inside these barriers impedes discussion and understanding of the curriculum offerings even within the discipline. . . . If faculty members are to accept academic advising as a really important function, they are going to have to spend time on it, and administrative officials are going to have to recognize that time is necessary."

A number of questions can be raised about advisers and advising in any institution: (1) To what extent are advisers informed and up to date on programs, procedures, and requirements? If there are deficiencies, how can they be remedied? This point has two dimensions: How can new advisers be educated about institutional programs, procedures, and requirements; and how can veteran advisers be updated effectively? Does the institution have an updated handbook for advisers? (2) Are advisers accessible? What procedures for arranging appointments seem to be most effective? (3) How does an institution identify those who are most interested in advising and who are most effective at it? (4) How does an institution work toward providing every student with at least one faculty member with whom he can discuss problems and concerns? (5) What institutional procedures are needed to ensure that new advisers are promptly appointed to replace those who leave, and how are students informed of the new advisers? Sometimes permanent advisers are assigned to freshmen so late that much confusion exists during the early weeks of the academic term. (6) What are the

41

responsibilities and authority of the adviser? (7) What procedures can an institution initiate to reduce the possibilities of students' discovering graduation deficiencies at the last minute? (8) What recognition is given to the time and expertise required for effective advising? Should everyone have an advising load even if he has little interest or competence in this area?

The institutional response to this problem is critical. Ideally, released time or diminished academic load should be given for ad-visee loads, and some colleges and universities have worked out such procedures. Hardee describes some innovative approaches: "At Bradley University, sixteen freshmen advisers assigned fifty coun-selees each are freed of two periods of instruction a week. At New Jersey State Teachers College, a counseling hour is a scheduled weekly event, and during that hour no classes are conducted. At Stephens College, advising days are designated at several times during the academic year, with classes suspended in order that (1) advisers and students meet in conference and (2) advisers have adequate time to write the letters to parents which are required" (1959, pp. 108–109).

The number of advisees that can be effectively counseled by one faculty member varies according to the faculty member's ability and style, the subject area, the year level of the student, the number of students in the program, personal preferences of students, adjust-ment problems of the student, and the general style of the institution, including, of course, its emphasis on counseling.

There is no one best way to adjust academic load to advisee load or to assign advisees to faculty members. As a starting point, each institution will need to examine its commitment to the advising and counseling program; organization and procedure should follow from the basic philosophical and policy commitment. This commit-ment, if more than rhetoric, should be measurable. The student ap-praisal forms on page 45 are one means to this end.

Since the faculty members' advising functions may be divided into two broad categories—academic advising and personal coun-seling—the appraisal form takes both into consideration. Whether one or both are used will depend upon a number of factors that will need to be decided by each institution.

Application of procedure. The appraisal instrument for advising or counseling effectiveness may be administered to advisees at the end of each term or perhaps once per academic year. The completed forms can be placed in a large envelope by the instructor, sealed, and passed on to the office of the dean or to the department chairman, depending upon the procedure that has been adopted by the institution.

Composite rating. Total the responses that are used and divide this total by six, twelve, or whatever number of items are used. For example, professor A has a gross score of 40 on the six items in the academic advising section. This figure divided by six comes to 6.7, which is the composite rating of professor A on academic advising. Professor B, for example, has a gross score of 76 because the students rated him on both academic advising and personal counseling. Seventy-six divided by twelve equals 6.3, which is the composite rating of professor B on the two scales.

FACULTY SERVICE AND RELATIONS

The academic community is a very human one, and in this respect it probably is no more or less controlled by human feelings than business or government. It is a well known generalization, substantiated by various research studies, that human frailties rather than technical inadequacies account for most of the severances in business and industry. Some scholars like to believe, in spite of evidence to the contrary, that the subjective is not a prominent factor in evaluation of faculty performance. In his study of faculty evaluation at 584 institutions, Gustad found that the "personal attributes" category figured prominently in evaluation, as indicated in Table 4. One will notice that the "other" category was second in importance. Gustad mentions that this item was used frequently to deal with such factors as cooperation, loyalty, Christian character, church membership and activity, and compatibility—all of which could have been included under "personal attributes." If this factor, the third highest in the overall ratings, is combined with the "other"

Table 4. Factors Considered in Evaluating Faculty Members

TYPE OF INSTITUTION

Factor	Liberal Arts Colleges		Private Universities		State Universities		State Colleges		Teachers Colleges		Junior Colleges		Professional and Technical Colleges		Total	
	Mean	Rank	Mean	Rank	Mean	Rank	Mean	Rank	Mean	Rank	Mean	Rank	Mean	Rank	Mean	Rank
Classroom teaching	2.97	1	2.96	1	2.91	1.0	3.00	1.5	2.97	2.0	3.00	1	2.95	1	2.97	1
Supervision of graduate study	.94	13	1.70	10	2.35	5.0	1.42	11.0	1.42	11.0	.13	14	1.55	11	1.36	11
Supervision of honors	1.14	12	1.25	13	1.35	12.0	.90	14.0	.86	14.0	.57	12	.61	14	.95	14
Research	2.02	8	2.53	3	2.82	2.0	1.95	8.5	1.66	10.0	.78	10	2.31	3	2.02	5
Publication	2.08	6	2.41	4	2.70	4.0	1.95	8.5	1.76	8.5	.96	9	2.21	5	2.01	6
Public service	1.72	10	1.54	11	1.77	9.5	1.79	10.0	1.79	7.0	1.61	8	1.68	10	1.70	10
Consultation	.93	14	1.22	14	1.31	13.5	1.22	12.0	1.24	12.0	.52	13	1.37	12	1.12	12
Professional society activity	2.00	9	1.88	7	1.86	7.5	2.04	6.0	1.83	6.0	1.65	7	1.92	7	1.88	8
Student advising	2.40	4	2.21	5	1.86	7.5	2.37	4.0	2.14	4.0	2.52	4	1.95	6	2.21	4
Committee work	2.03	7	1.87	8	1.77	9.5	2.14	5.0	1.93	5.0	2.09	5	1.84	8	1.95	7
Length of service in rank	2.17	5	1.82	9	1.45	11.0	1.98	7.0	1.76	8.5	1.78	6	1.76	9	1.82	9
Competing offers	1.19	11	1.35	12	1.31	13.5	1.03	13.0	.93	13.0	.70	11	1.08	13	1.08	13
Personal attributes	2.49	3	2.15	6	1.98	6.0	2.49	3.0	2.28	3.0	2.61	3	2.29	4	2.33	3
Other	2.91	2	2.57	2	2.86	3.0	3.00	1.5	3.00	1.0	2.86	2	2.88	2	2.87	2
Total Mean	1.93		1.96		2.02		1.95		1.83		1.56		1.89		1.88	
Total Variance	4.13		4.11		4.44		4.19		3.71		3.27		3.93		3.87	

Source: Gustad, 1961.

Name of adviser .... Date ....

STUDENT APPRAISAL OF ADVISING

Please fill in the name of your faculty adviser or counselor (whoever signs your class schedule) and also the date.

This survey is given to learn about how you view your adviser. Please do not sign your name. The space at the end of the survey allows you to use your own words, and extra questions may be added. Your assistance is appreciated.

Directions:

The appraisal instrument is divided into two sections: (A) Academic Advising, and (B) Personal Counseling. Section B is to be used only if you have had personal counseling—if personal counseling is an acknowledged aspect of student advising.

Each statement describes a basic component of advising and/or counseling. Rate your adviser on each item, giving the highest scores for unusually effective performances. Place in the blank space before each statement the number that most nearly expresses your view:

Highest			Average			Lowest	Don't Know
7	6	5	4	3	2	1	X

A. Academic Advising

.... 1. Advises in terms of alternatives and encourages you to assume responsibility for decisions.
.... 2. Has personal interest in assisting you through advising.
.... 3. Keeps appointments when made in advance.
.... 4. Keeps up-to-date with regulations and course offerings.
.... 5. Maintains accurate files on your progress.
.... 6. Seeks to plan programs consistent with your stated objectives.
.... 7.
.... 8.

B. Personal Counseling (Answer these questions if personal counseling is an acknowledged aspect of student advising.)

.... 1. Able to start working towards a solution to your problems because of this counseling.
.... 2. Is helpful to you.
.... 3. Is objective and non-punitive.
.... 4. Is willing to use college or community resources when your problems seem to be more than he could handle.
.... 5. Understands your point of view.
.... 6. Would you wish to return to this counselor for help in the future?
.... 7.
.... 8.
.... Composite rating.

45

category, it becomes the second most important factor after class-room teaching (1961). (Also see Gustad, 1967.) Because personal considerations do, in fact, enter into faculty evaluations, criteria need to be developed that reflect this aspect and allow some measurement of it.

An important distinction should be made between academic freedom and academic responsibility. The professor's right to differ, to challenge, and to question is at the heart of the collegiate enterprise and should be defended vigorously. At the same time, "respect for the opinion of others" is recognized in both the 1940 AAUP statement on academic freedom and the 1970 AAUP statement on "freedom and responsibility." The latter statement goes farther than other AAUP documents in spelling out responsible behavior as it relates to academic freedom. In other words, when appraising faculty relations, one needs to differentiate between *what* one says and *how* one says it. The right to academic freedom carries with it the obligation of civility toward one's colleagues and others.

The category of faculty service and relations should be helpful in determining the amount of time that a faculty member spends in classroom-related activities. A few professors make college and university service and relations their first order of business, and their classroom teaching suffers. The Peter Principle (mediocrity seeks its highest level of incompetence) does apply to some professors who occupy positions of influence in internal institutional governance systems, particularly in the large universities. For these individuals internal governance activities have taken the place of serious teaching, research, scholarly study, or writing.

Most faculty members, however, will be involved to some degree with service activities; such involvement is generally necessary and also usually helpful. The department chairman is ordinarily in the best position to rate this involvement (see appraisal form on page 47), and faculty members can be asked for a self-evaluation in this area for comparison with departmental appraisal.

Composite rating. Total the ratings on all items used and divide this figure by five, seven, or whatever number of items are used. For example, professor A has a gross score of 32 on five items.

FACULTY SERVICE AND RELATIONS APPRAISAL

Name of teacher _____ Year _____

Appraiser _____ Title _____

Directions:

Please write in the blank space the number that describes your judgment of that factor as it relates to an individual's faculty service and relations. Rate the individual on each item, giving the highest scores for unusually effective performances. Additional questions may be added.

Highest			Average			Lowest	Don't Know
7	6	5	4	3	2	1	X

_____ 1. Acceptance of college assignments. Does he accept college assignments willingly? Does he volunteer occasionally?

_____ 2. Attitude. Does he act in the best interests of the department and the college? Does he take a professional attitude toward human relations and personnel problems? Does he have a positive attitude?

_____ 3. Cooperation. To what extent does the faculty member assist colleagues and others with their problems? Is he a good team member?

_____ 4. Performance on college assignments. What is his performance level? How do colleagues perceive his performance?

_____ 5. Professional behavior as it relates to his professional activities and the goals and nature of the institution. Does he act responsibly?

_____ 6.

_____ 7.

_____ Composite rating.

Description of specific faculty assignments and services: _____

_____

_____

Comments: _____

_____

_____

47

This figure divided by five is 6.4, representing the composite score of professor A on faculty service and relations. Professor B has a gross score of 35 on six items (including one write-in item). Thirty-five divided by six comes to 5.8, which is the composite score of professor B.

MANAGEMENT (ADMINISTRATION)

The quality of management is a key to the success of any institutionalized enterprise. According to a *Forbes* magazine (September 15, 1968, pp. 51–52) study, "the clear lesson of fifty action-packed years of U.S. business history" is this: "If a company has nothing going for it except one thing—good management—it will make the grade. If it has every thing *except* good management, it will flop."

With respect to the higher education enterprise two aspects of management are considered: administration related to the performance of professional activities such as teaching and research; and part- or full-time administration. Referring to professional administrative activities, a faculty advisory committee at The Ohio State University found that administrative functions absorbed greater blocks of time than previously supposed, and that these functions were related to each major activity undertaken by the faculty member. In discussing research, for example, the committee reported that administrative activities include "the non-technical aspects of the preparation of research proposals, the selling of proposals to sponsors, attendance at conferences with sponsors, making arrangements for travel, personnel-management, cost-accounting, procurement of building-space, procurement of equipment, procurement of materials and supplies, sub-contracting, report preparation, etc., all related to research. It also includes service on policy-making committees having to do with research, and the administrative aspects of integrating research with teaching. Although central administrative offices help with some of these tasks, the bulk of such work can only be done by the professors" (1967, p. 5). While such administrative duties require more time than generally supposed, it is usually not practical to reduce faculty load.

Evaluation should include all levels of academe—the president, vice-presidents, deans, and department chairmen in addition to the faculty and teaching assistants. Presidential evaluation should be the primary responsibility of the board of trustees although the board might want to devise ways and means to gain evidence from other clienteles. The procedures for the various levels will need to be adapted to the style and nature of each institution, but the principle of evaluation—from top to bottom—should be followed. In all cases, evaluation should be viewed, and used, primarily as a means of improving performance.

The procedure for using the administrative appraisal instrument on page 50 should be worked out by each institution according to its style and nature. Administrative evaluation standards should be developed along with those for faculty evaluation. In other words, is the overall rating of 6.1 for teaching equivalent to the 6.1 overall rating for the college dean? This, and several other questions, will need to be researched, but the concept and practice of systematic administrative evaluation should become more evident in the future.

Composite rating. Total the ratings on all items used and then divide this figure by the number of items used. For examples, see this subheading in the section on advising or faculty service and relations.

PERFORMING AND VISUAL ARTS

This category is evidence of the increasing importance of the performing and visual arts in developing wise, compassionate, and perceptive individuals. The arts can make the major contribution in developing perception and understanding, in learning that works experienced visually (architecture, sculpture, and painting) can be a significant aspect of learning and knowing, and in realizing that the study of performing and visual arts is an academic discipline in its own right. But "the arts can win priority on the agenda of American higher education in the 1970s only by concerted action" (Dennis and Jacob, 1968, p. 139).

"Performing and visual arts" includes recitals, concerts, and public lectures; musical, theatrical, and dance productions; and

ADMINISTRATIVE EFFECTIVENESS APPRAISAL

Name of administrator .... Year ....

Appraiser .... Title ....

Directions:

Write the number in the blank space that describes your judgment of that factor. Rate the administrator on each item that is appropriate, giving the highest scores for unusually effective performances. The blank numbers allow for two additional items, and the space at the end of the survey allows for a narrative description.

							Don't
Highest			Average			Lowest	Know
7	6	5	4	3	2	1	X

.... 1. Ability and willingness to "open doors" for faculty members.

.... 2. Attends to details effectively.

.... 3. Instills enthusiasm for professional goals.

.... 4. Judges people perceptively and fairly.

.... 5. Keeps abreast of new developments and innovations in higher education.

.... 6. Makes sound decisions.

.... 7. Plans effectively and imaginatively.

.... 8. Resolves or ameliorates human conflicts.

.... 9. Says "no" effectively.

.... 10. Understands and uses modern management procedures.

.... 11. Willingness to appraise situations and problems impartially.

.... 12. Willingness to put others first.

.... 13. Works effectively with faculty members.

.... 14. Works effectively with other administrators.

.... 15.

.... 16.

.... Composite rating.

50

exhibitions of paintings, sculptures, and other creative works. Teachers in the creative arts present a particular problem in terms of evaluation. Staging a theatrical production, for example, combines something of classroom teaching, management, public service, and research; yet it does not fit in any one of them. And, while the time and effort invested may be great, the quantity of works will probably be limited. A choral director, for example, may have as his major responsibility the production of Christmas and Easter presentations. A category such as "performing and visual arts" is needed not only to provide recognition of such endeavors in college and university life, but also to provide a basis on which to judge them. The appraisal form on page 52 proposes two types of evaluation. The first is a self-evaluation of the production, performance, or exhibition, and the second is an appraisal by the department chairman or the appropriate administrative officer.

Application of procedure. The department chairman studies the self-evaluation form and gathers information relative to the five or more criteria on the quantified form. Views of students may not be sought in a systematic way unless the chairman wants input from a few key student participants.

Composite rating. Total the ratings on all items used and then divide this figure by the number of items used. For examples, see this subheading in the section on advising or faculty service and relations. The percentage of professional load given to this category should be determined by the department chairman in consultation with the faculty member. Many options are possible; a few might be:

A		B		C	
advising	10%	p and v arts	100%	p and v arts	30%
teaching	60			professional status	20
p and v arts	30			administration	50
	100%				100%

PROFESSIONAL STATUS AND ACTIVITIES

The basic content and procedures in any discipline change rapidly—a matter of two or three years in some fields and five or six years in others. Keeping abreast of such changes is the positive

PERFORMING AND VISUAL ARTS

1. Self-Evaluation

Teacher .... Date ....

Title of presentation ....

Place or occasion of presentation ....

Time spent on this project ....

.... 1. Describe the presentation, including a statement of your
intention or purpose. ....

.... 2. Discuss briefly any special difficulties that you encountered
in producing the work or in making arrangements for its
presentation or exhibition. ....

.... 3. Were other faculty members or students included in this
production, performance, or exhibition project? If so, who
and to what extent? ....

.... 4. How was the work received by the audience or the spectators? ....

.... 5. How was the work received by the critics?

.... 6. Do you think the reaction of the audience or spectators
and the reaction of the critics were justifiable in terms of
your stated intentions for the project?

.... 7. How did you feel about this production or exhibition?

Other comments: ....

PERFORMING AND VISUAL ARTS

2. Quantified Appraisal

Teacher .... Date ....

Appraiser .... Title ....

Directions:

In rating each activity, highest scores are for unusually effective performances. Place in the blank space before each statement the number that most nearly expresses your view. Additional items may be included, and the space at the end of the survey allows a narrative statement.

Highest			Average			Lowest	Don't Know
7	6	5	4	3	2	1	X

.... 1. Judgments of colleagues.

.... 2. Judgments of other professionals.

.... 3. Self-appraisal (by director of production).

.... 4. Tenor of newspaper review.

.... 5. Views of students.

.... 6.

.... 7.

.... Composite rating.

Nature of performance: ....

....

....

Additional comments: ....

....

....

side of professional status and activities; using the campus as a base for professional operations or as a postage stamp is the negative side. (It is said that one large university has three faculties: one flying in, one flying out, and one on the campus; and of another that the most likely place to meet fellow faculty members is in Washington.) In recent years many universities employed "name" professors at high salaries, furnishing them with expense accounts, special secretarial assistance, and virtual autonomy over their activities in the belief that their professional status and activities would bring prestige and credit to the institution. It has worked out this way in some instances; in others the professor has coasted or the project that gave him notoriety has become obsolete. With the passing of the bull market in higher education—at least for some years—one can expect to see marked diminution in the buying of name professors as a means of obtaining instant institutional prestige.

It is unlikely that all seven criteria listed on the appraisal form (page 55) will apply to every individual. What may be desired from those with several years of academic performance can hardly be expected from less experienced faculty. Decisions about appropriate categories should be made by the individual faculty member in consultation with the department head. Department chairmen need to have individual folders available so various pieces of information can be filed at that moment, or other written procedures will be needed so the chairman can stay abreast with activities of the faculty member.

Composite rating. Total the ratings on all items used, and then divide this figure by the number of items used. For examples, see this subheading in the section on advising or faculty service and relations.

PUBLICATIONS

Publication is generally subsumed under research, but this practice is gross in that it fails to take into account many of the idiosyncracies of this area. Some important studies are never published commercially, such as final reports of special projects. The

PROFESSIONAL STATUS AND ACTIVITIES APPRAISAL

Professor .... Date ....

Appraiser .... Title ....

Directions:

An individual should be rated on each item that is appropriate for him, giving the highest scores for unusually effective performances. Additional items and narrative comments can be included.

Highest			Average			Lowest	Don't Know
7	6	5	4	3	2	1	X

.... 1. Activity in professional associations and societies. (which ones) ....

....

.... 2. Offices in professional associations and societies. (which ones) ....

....

.... 3. Papers or other presentations before professional groups. (what papers and which groups) ....

....

.... 4. Evidences of efforts toward individual professional improvement (elaborate if necessary).

....

....

.... 5. Professional status, as viewed by colleagues. ....

....

.... 6. Professional status, as viewed by the profession. ....

.... 7. Professional recognition in terms of awards or honors. (state which ones) ....

....

.... 8.

.... 9.

.... Composite rating.

55

division between publications and research, for example, can be fuzzy in that most research studies eventually become publications yet many publications are not based upon research. One can argue that facilitating basic and applied research is more important to the university than facilitating publication. Without entering into this polemical area, one can say that the production of publications —whether based upon research, upon theoretical considerations, upon philosophical logic or upon other academically respectable bases—is an important area for evaluation.

Counting only so-called "refereed" journals as bona fide periodical publications is not recommended because some excellent periodicals are not refereed. A decision about an article should be based upon the quality of both the article and the journal rather than solely in terms of the journal's refereed or non-refereed status. Again, as with the other eight categories, the weight given to the publication category is an individual and departmental matter. The weight given to publications can vary from zero to 100 percent, according to agreed-upon professional workload.

Gustad inquired about the procedures used for evaluating publications (see Table 5). While this study is more than ten years old, there is no reason to believe that the procedures have changed much.

In discussing these findings, Gustad noted that "faculty yardage—the resume or publications list and the reprints sown in strategic places—is the principal basis for evaluation. It would appear that colleagues, chairmen, and deans are the ones who evaluate this material. *Some* chairmen, *some* colleagues, and a *few* deans are probably capable of doing so" (1961, p. 14). Because of their second- or third-hand position, deans normally should have a minimal role in directly evaluating these categories, but they do have a major role in putting together the pieces and in making the final decision. (This is discussed further in the final chapter.)

The five categories of publications are: books; monographs; special reports, including those written for the college as well as for other groups and organizations; chapters in books; and periodical articles. Appraisal forms for all categories may be found on pages 58–62.

Table 5. DATA GATHERED FOR EVALUATING PUBLICATION

Types of Institutions, by Percentages

Source	Liberal Arts Colleges	Private Universities	State Universities	State Colleges	Teachers Colleges	Junior Colleges	Technical Professional Colleges
Faculty résumé	28	37	50	28	48	28	42
Committee evaluation	2	22	17	6	10	0	5
National reputation	3	15	17	2	4	0	3
On-campus reputation	10	13	17	2	7	0	5
Journal quality	8	12	10	8	0	0	8
Chairman evaluation	10	18	30	14	7	0	18
Dean evaluation	22	13	30	14	10	0	18
Reprints	32	21	27	34	24	8	24
Other	2	0	3	6	7	0	0

Source: Gustad, 1961.

BOOK APPRAISAL

Professor .... Date ....

Appraiser .... Title ....

Directions:

Place in the blank spaces before each statement the number that most nearly expresses your finding. Additional statements and comments may be added.

Highest			Average			Lowest	Don't Know
7	6	5	4	3	2	1	X

Each book (Title, publisher, number of pages, date, or list contract signed and make a progress report if writing is underway)

....

....

....

.... 1. Generally speaking, how does the publisher rate in this particular field?

.... 2. How do colleagues within the department generally rate the publication?

.... 3. How do colleagues outside the institution rate the publication?

.... 4. How does the department chairman rate the publication?

.... 5. How has the book been reviewed?

.... 6. Has the book been cited or quoted?

.... 7. How does the author rate the book?

.... 8.

.... 9.

.... Composite rating on book (total score ÷ number of items used).

Comments: ....

....

58

MONOGRAPH APPRAISAL

Name .... Date ....

Appraiser .... Title ....

Each Monograph (Description):

....

....

....

....

....

.... 1. Generally speaking, how does the publisher rate in this particular field?

.... 2. How do colleagues within the department generally rate the publication?

.... 3. How do colleagues outside the institution rate the publication?

.... 4. How does the department chairman rate the publication?

.... 5. How has the monograph been reviewed?

.... 6. Has the monograph been cited or quoted?

.... 7. How does the author rate the book?

.... 8.

.... 9.

.... Composite rating on monograph (total score ÷ number of items used).

Comments: ....

....

....

....

....

SPECIAL REPORT APPRAISAL

Name .... Date ....

Appraiser .... Title ....

Each Special Report:

....

....

....

....

.... 1. Generally speaking, how does the publisher rate in this particular field?

.... 2. How do colleagues within the department generally rate the report?

.... 3. How do colleagues outside the institution rate the publication?

.... 4. How does the department chairman rate the publication?

.... 5. How has the report been reviewed?

.... 6. Has the special report been cited or quoted?

.... 7. How does the author rate the report?

.... 8.

.... 9.

.... Composite rating on special report (total score ÷ number of items used).

Comments: ....

....

....

....

CHAPTER-IN-BOOK APPRAISAL

Name .... Date ....

Appraiser .... Title ....

Chapter in Books:

....

....

....

....

.... 1. Generally speaking, how does the publisher rate in this particular field?

.... 2. How do colleagues within the department rate the chapter?

.... 3. How do colleagues outside the institution rate the chapter?

.... 4. How does the department chairman rate the chapter?

.... 5. How has the chapter been reviewed?

.... 6. Has the chapter been cited or quoted?

.... 7. How does the author rate the chapter?

.... 8.

.... 9.

.... Composite rating on chapter (total score ÷ number of items used).

Comments: ....

....

....

....

61

PERIODICAL ARTICLE APPRAISAL

Name .... Date ....

Appraiser .... Title ....

Each Periodical Article:

....

....

....

.... 1. Generally speaking, how does the publisher rate in this particular field?

.... 2. How do colleagues within the department rate the article?

.... 3. How do colleagues outside the institution rate the article?

.... 4. How does the department chairman rate the article?

.... 5. How has the article been reviewed?

.... 6. Has the article been cited or quoted?

.... 7. How does the author view the article?

.... 8.

.... 9.

.... Composite rating on article (Total score ÷ number of items used).

Comments: ....

....

....

....

....

More Than a Teacher

Both quantity and quality should be taken into consideration when evaluating publications. While it is obvious that two quality articles should receive more institutional recognition than one, two relatively minor pieces may not merit the attention of one outstanding article. The time required to complete an individual work also needs to be considered in the evaluation. The final weighing is determined by the department chairman in consultation with the individual faculty member.

Composite rating. If an individual is to be rated at all in the category of publications, the total criterion effort should total 100, regardless of the weight that is given the publication category in the overall professional load. The following figures indicate three variations.

Professor A

Publications	Composite Rating	Percentage of Publication Effort		Raw Score	Overall Rating
book	6.2	×	100	= 620	.89
monograph					
special report					
chapter					
periodical					

(overall rating = raw score ÷ 700)

Professor B

Publications	Composite Rating	Percentage of Publication Effort		Raw Score	Overall Rating
book					
monograph	6.0	×	40	= 240	
special report					
chapter	5.8	×	30	= 174	
periodical	6.3	×	30	= 189	
			100	603	.86

(603 ÷ 700 = .86)

Professor C

Publications	Composite Rating	Percentage of Publication Effort		Raw Score	Overall Rating
book					
monograph					
special report					
chapter					
periodical	6.3	×	100	= 630	.90

PUBLIC SERVICE

For purposes of evaluation, public service and professional activities are usually lumped together, or public and university services are combined. Such procedures do not allow sufficient differentiation. Some university professors in agriculture, for example, have much use for a public service category. In other instances, activities are performed as a service to the community and/or some other geographical area. Working with community groups, serving on statewide or national committees, and working with poverty groups would be examples of this service.

Public service that develops from one's professional competence would consume a major segment of time for only a very few faculty members, but the category does provide a means of recognizing the growing social consciousness among college professors and a precise appraisal of those who do have some professional activity in these areas. In order to count public service as a professional activity, however, it should relate to one's profession. Boy scout leadership, community chest activities, and political campaign participation, for example—all worthy uses of time—represent voluntary exercise or civic responsibilities unrelated to one's professional activities; therefore, they would not be included in the public service category. The form for appraising profession-related public service will be found on page 67.

Procedure for evaluation. Gustad inquired about the procedures used for evaluating public service, with the results indicated in Table 6. In analyzing the responses, Gustad (1961, pp. 14–15) notes that "again the ubiquitous faculty resume is high on the list; that is, the faculty members tell someone, usually the chairman or dean, what they have been doing. This presumably is about as informative as a publications list. From it, one knows that the faculty member is not entirely cloistered and that someone is presumably interested enough in him to invite (or permit) him to venture into the market place." The department chairman is ordinarily responsible for gathering evidence from the professor, his colleagues, students, outside evaluators, and possibly others, and whenever necessary he should discuss aspects of the assignment with the individual. The area of public service, admittedly difficult to appraise, can be evaluated through systematic and planned effort.

Composite rating. Total the ratings on all items used, and then divide this figure by the number of items used. For examples, see this subheading in the section on advising or faculty service and relations.

RESEARCH

The definition of research used in this report is taken from the *Handbook of Research on Teaching,* published by the American Educational Research Association, which defines research as "activity aimed at increasing our power to understand, predict, and control events of a given kind" (1963, p. 97). And in judging the validity of including some activities as aspects of the research continuum, we were guided by a special report for the *Handbook* by Clark, Hilgard, and Humphreys, in which research was divided into six categories: basic scientific investigation, content indifferent; basic scientific investigation, content relevant; investigations of educationally oriented problems; classroom experimentation; field testing, and installing the materials widely (1963, pp. 97–98). Such categorization is necessary in order to deal with the greatly varying ways of knowing and learning that are found among the academic disciplines. Some institutions attach an unwritten priority to research in one area or cluster of areas, and this of course is their prerogative,

Table 6. DATA COLLECTED FOR EVALUATING PUBLIC SERVICE

	Types of Institutions, by Percentages						
Source	Liberal Arts Colleges	Private Universities	State Universities	State Colleges	Teachers Colleges	Junior Colleges	Technical-Professional Colleges
Faculty résumé	30	37	67	42	48	36	34
Faculty committee	0	4	3	2	7	0	3
Chairman evaluation	10	21	20	4	17	4	13
Dean evaluation	10	10	23	6	10	0	11
Public reaction	5	9	3	10	4	0	3
Public relations office	18	6	13	18	7	24	11
Nature of the organization	0	2	3	0	4	0	3
General knowledge	18	9	10	12	7	12	0
Other	0	6	3	6	7	0	0

Source: Gustad, 1961.

PUBLIC SERVICE APPRAISAL

Professor .... Date ....

Appraiser .... Title ....

Nature of service:

....

....

....

Time involved:
Some quantitive appraisal should be made of the professional time spent. The portion of time given to public service, growing out of consultation between the individual and the department chairman, should be calculated as carefully as possible.

....

| 100% | 90 | 80 | 70 | 60 | 50 | 40 | 30 | 20 | 10 | 0% |

Directions:
Place in the blank spaces before each statement the number that most nearly expresses your finding. Additional items and comments may be added.

	Highest			Average			Lowest	Don't Know
	7	6	5	4	3	2	1	X

.... 1. Contribution of service: What is the value of the service, as judged by those who receive it and as can be best ascertained by the department chairman?

.... 2. Quality of performance: This criterion relates to the previous one but its appraisal should come primarily from colleagues and those professionals who can judge the quality of the individual's professional contribution.

.... 3.

.... 4.

.... Composite rating.

Comments: ....

....

....

67

but such an arrangement can cause difficulties in the evaluation procedure. A frank approach to the matter of priorities is preferable.

The matter of basic versus applied research may also pose a problem. The balance between the two is always tenuous and difficult for any particular institution to judge. The hierarchy of importance is an institutional matter, and the *quality* of what is done should be the dominant factor. The *relevance* of what is done should be determined in terms of institutional and departmental priorities. In a period of tight money, basic research is most likely to suffer financial cuts—a tendency that can have serious long range repercussions on the development of various technologies.

The research-versus-teaching controversy is hardly a new concern, but, unfortunately, all the heat it has generated has not produced its equivalent in light. "Hard" research on the relationship between teaching and research—the publish-or-perish syndrome—is scarce, but from what is available one can make the following generalization: In medium and large institutions of higher education, good researchers are good teachers. Or to put it another way, good teachers who do very little or no research are the exception rather than the rule. In their study of research versus teaching, Jencks and Riesman "found no evidence . . . that the two are antagonistic. Teachers cannot remain stimulating unless they also continue to learn, and while this learning may not focus on small, manageable 'research problems,' it is research by any reasonable definition. When a teacher stops doing it, he begins to repeat himself and eventually loses touch with both the young and the world around him. . . . The 'research-teaching' dilemma is, then, a false one. The real problem is to marry the two enterprises" (1969, pp. 532–33).

What is true for medium and large institutions may not apply, however, to small ones—the private, liberal arts colleges with enrollments under one thousand. These institutions often require heavier teaching loads and may provide less encouragement for research in terms of both administrative and material support. Yet the benefits of more or less continuous literature review and interpretation of research and new theories may be more important to the professor in a small liberal arts college who wants to keep on top of his field. It is very important that these colleges have special summer faculty development programs and other in-year opportunities to keep abreast.

Procedure for evaluation. Gustad inquired about the procedures used for evaluating research, with the results indicated in Table 7: The faculty resume, as was the case for publications and public service, remains the most frequently cited procedure, with the opinions of colleagues, chairmen, and deans as the most prominent external sources. In the "other" category, the most frequently mentioned device consisted in counting citations to a professor's work in other publications (Gustad, 1961, pp. 13–14).

Research may be either ongoing or completed. Since some research requires two or more years to complete, a yearly appraisal is desirable. Research appraisal has two aspects: a self-appraisal and a more quantified appraisal form for others to complete (see page 71, 72). Chairmen are responsible for securing appraisals from appropriate individuals, including the researcher. Admittedly, the quality and promise of research are difficult to judge, but most current procedures cannot be justified. Too often the size of the research project is directly related to the quality of the product— the larger the project the better it is. Systematic use of criteria can help guard against the tendency to equate quantity with quality, and it can also assist in providing fairer judgment of smaller, non-supported research.

Composite rating. Total the ratings on all items used, and then divide this figure by the number of items used. For examples, see this subheading in the section on advising or faculty service and relations.

Table 7. Data Gathered for Evaluating Research

Types of Institutions, by Percentages

Source	Liberal Arts Colleges	Private Universities	State Universities	State Colleges	Teachers Colleges	Junior Colleges	Technical-Professional Colleges
Faculty résumé	35	38	50	40	45	20	45
Faculty committees	2	24	13	2	10	0	3
National reputation	3	19	23	4	4	0	8
Journal quality	2	3	13	0	0	0	0
Contracts and grants	8	9	23	2	10	0	8
Chairman evaluation	15	24	37	20	17	4	16
Dean evaluation	20	15	30	16	14	0	18
Research proposals	5	7	7	4	14	0	11
Research committees	5	7	3	6	4	0	13
On-campus reputation	15	15	20	12	7	0	21
Other	3	3	0	2	10	0	0

Source: Gustad, 1961.

RESEARCH

1. Self-Evaluation

Professor .... Date ....

Directions:

The individual undertaking, or having completed, the research should fill in this form. (Use additional pages wherever necessary.)

1. Nature of research project. ....
   ....

2. Are/were the goals of the project well defined? ....

3. Are/were these goals realistic with respect to time and resources? ....

4. Which obstacles have been overcome? How was this achieved?
   ....

5. Which resources have you found most available and useful?
   ....

6. Which resources did you find lacking? ....

7. Has the college community been receptive to your work?
   ....

8. Have your colleagues taken an active interest in your research?
   ....

9. Has the research changed, modified, or enhanced the direction of your theoretical position? ....

10. If students were involved, what were their reactions toward the project? ....

11. What are your plans regarding publication? ....
    ....

71

RESEARCH

2. Quantified Appraisal

Professor .... Date ....

Appraiser .... Title ....

Status of research:

completed ....

ongoing .... (when started) ....

Nature of research:

(Brief description, or attached outline of it)

....

....

....

Time involved:

What proportion of your professional time was spent on this project?

....

| 100% | 90 | 80 | 70 | 60 | 50 | 40 | 30 | 20 | 10 | 0% |

Directions:

Place in the blank spaces before each statement the number that most nearly expresses your finding.

Highest			Average			Lowest	Don't Know
7	6	5	4	3	2	1	X

.... 1. How do colleagues within the department generally rate the research?

.... 2. How do colleagues outside the institution rate the research?

.... 3. How has the report been reviewed?

.... 4. Has the research been cited or quoted?

.... 5. How does the author rate the research?

.... 6.

.... 7.

.... Composite rating.

Comments: ....

....

....

72

Chapter 4

Determining Overall Performance Rating

[This book] . . . is called *The Art of Teaching* because I believe teaching is an art, not a science. It seems very dangerous to me to apply the aims and methods of science to human beings as individuals. . . . Teaching is not like inducing a chemistry reaction: it is much more like painting a picture, or making a piece of music, or on a lower level like planting a garden or writing a friendly letter. You must throw your heart into it, you must realize that it cannot be done by formulas, or you will spoil your work, and your pupils and yourself [Highet, 1950, from preface].

*T*hose who have spent many years in the classroom intuitively empathize with the eloquent pleadings of an eminent scholar, and he makes a fundamental point: human beings cannot be quantified. The human brain is one of nature's most marvelous inventions, and its intricacies and mysteries are just beginning to be understood. Coupled with man's emotions, one can appreciate Shakespeare's thought: "What a piece of work is a man."

And yet Donne wrote, "No man is an island, entire of itself."

We live in social contexts and we are judged according to some standard and by someone. While evaluation has developed very rapidly during this half of the twentieth century, it is conceivable that the "final" system of evaluation will not be developed in the foreseeable future, considering human complexities. Yet research and development have moved the field of evaluation much closer to respectability in terms of reliability and validity. Some fairly firm conclusions can be drawn from evaluation, and reliability can be determined. The other alternative is much less desirable: it is the rejection of what we do know about research and evaluation in favor of second-hand and/or intuitive judgment. In an age of science, the "art" of teaching must be respected, but the "science" of pedagogy is becoming more sensitive, adaptable, and precise.

ANNUAL RESUME OF ACTIVITIES

The faculty resume or yearly accounting of professional activities, sometimes known as "the brag sheet," is commonplace. Administrative officers do need a record of this sort, and it should be accumulated on a systematic basis. There is much misuse of the resume, however. Too often it becomes the primary basis for decisions on promotion, tenure, and salary. Such usage ascribes a value to the resume that it was not designed to have. The research reported by Gustad (see Chapter Three) found that the "ubiquitous" resume figured prominently in evaluating performance in publications, public service, and research—and it probably is prominent in other areas as well.

The resume, however, can provide information that is not gleaned from other procedures. For example, an innovative teaching approach may have been tried, or perhaps many hours have been spent in working out a new advising procedure for the department. While such activities may show up on other forms, the resume's narrative account can add a better understanding. Data on the resumes can be used as supplementary information wherever appropriate in the nine categories of professional activities. Each year, then, in a specified way and at a specified time, each faculty member should complete a resume of his activities for the preceding academic year. It should be used in conjunction with other evaluative materials in determining overall academic performance.

A sample resume is given for student advising on page 76. The same basic questions apply to the other eight categories. The resume is short, open-ended, and designed to elicit supplementary material that will increase the evaluators' understanding and appraisal of professional performance.

ANNUAL PERFORMANCE REVIEW

Some institutions require yearly professional review conferences for faculty members, but most do not. There is a sort of unwritten assumption that tenured, full professors have reached their zenith as teachers and that little can be done, or is needed, to improve them. Furthermore, the institution's internal governance system more often than not is controlled by these same professors. But some systematic review procedure for senior faculty members— perhaps every other year—is highly desirable.

The basic purpose of the conference is the improvement of overall academic performance. The conference can be quite constructive, depending upon preparation made by the department chairman as well as the spirit of the occasion. The senior faculty members conceivably can benefit as much, or more, than others because they have fewer opportunities to receive honest feedback about their professional performance. The conference should have a flexible format, and it should be frank, both specific and general, probing, and positive. Anticipated outcomes of such a conference should be better understanding on the part of both faculty member and department chairman, and an analysis of performance that will include some things that are being done well and some "things to work on." The conference will not be easy or particularly pleasant for either party, but it can be an important dimension of professional improvement. (For a description of the conference procedure developed at Defiance College, see Karman, 1969.)

REQUIRED VS. VOLUNTARY EVALUATION

The question of required, campus-wide evaluation versus voluntary evaluation remains a sensitive one. The following outline

STUDENT ADVISING RÉSUMÉ

Name .... For Academic Year ....

Department .... Date ....

The advising résumé provides an opportunity for you to describe your activities in this area. Use additional pages if necessary.

1. What were your advising responsibilities? ....

....
....
....
....
....
....
....

2. Were there innovative, creative, or special aspects of your advising that you would like to mention? ....

....
....
....
....
....
....
....

3. Other comments (any special circumstances or problems that should be considered). ....

....
....
....
....
....
....
....

76

analyzes the advantages and disadvantages of required, campuswide evaluation.

Advantages. (1) Campus-wide evaluation allows cross comparison, making it possible to locate the stronger and weaker departments on the campus. Without such a system, effectiveness among the various units can only be guessed at. (2) Accountability is becoming a more prominent aspect of higher education, and colleges and universities need to take the initiative in developing evaluative procedures for measuring accountability before legislative aides do the job for them. Accountability includes a more precise reckoning of the relationship between resources allocated and results achieved. (3) Campus-wide evaluation can greatly improve the overall academic quality of the institution. Any voluntary system may well miss those units and individuals who most need to improve. (4) Campus-wide evaluation offers the possibility of fairer overall decision-making about academic personnel. A fairer basis for comparability of overall professional performance is possible (and this consideration is especially important when fiscal considerations require that an institution make difficult personnel and program decisions), the campus as a whole can become more sensitive and sophisticated in the procedures and application of evaluation.

Disadvantages. (1) The use of the same student appraisal form, as one example, for music and physics and philosophy and agriculture asks too much of the quantified instrument. The differences among various subject areas are too great to be spanned by a single instrument. (2) A campus-wide system requires an amount of time and money, if done properly, that many institutions are not willing to commit. They want the benefits without the cost. (3) Faculty morale can be adversely affected by a campus-wide system regardless of how well it is managed, and faculty morale will suffer substantially if a campus-wide system is poorly managed.

While other points can undoubtedly be made on either side of the argument, these should be sufficient to illustrate the sensitivities and difficulties of any campus-wide system that is required of all academic personnel. Do the advantages outweigh the disadvantages? In general, the answer is yes, but "in general" needs to be particularized if it is to have meaning at the local level. Several conditions need to be satisfied before any required, campus-wide system is seriously considered: the administration and a significant portion of the faculty should be in favor of such a system; sufficient human and material resources should be allocated to the project to allow effective management of it; and much forethought needs to be given to four matters: the procedures to be followed; sufficient standardization of the procedures to achieve campus-wide comparability (yet sufficient particularization so that individual programs and circumstances can be accommodated); who will interpret the results; and how these will be used.

EVALUATION FOR PROMOTION AND TENURE

Thus far this volume has not dealt with the uses of evaluation for promotion and tenure. The primary purpose of systematic evaluation should be for individual professional improvement. This purpose is not a palliative or a play on words; it recognizes the importance of systematically analyzing one's professional performance with the purpose of improving.

The data also should be used in making decisions about promotion and tenure. Tenure, if held for twenty-five years, represents a monetary investment in excess of $600,000 and an institutional commitment to the competencies and personality that the individual brings to the position. The future quality and direction of any institution require that the tenure decision be considered most carefully.

How are promotion and tenure decisions made? The process often begins with a letter from the department chairman to the college dean with a carbon to the faculty member (or the other way around) making known the eligibility of professor X for promotion and/or tenure. As a second step, the candidate submits evidence of his professional activities and competencies—the "brag" sheet. The chairman usually asks tenured members of the department for a confidential letter that appraises the candidate's professional performance. The tenured colleague may be asked to write on specified criteria such as teaching and research or he may be given carte blanche.

A word needs to be said about "support" letters for those who are eligible for promotion and tenure. In many cases these letters have little value as analytical evidences of professional competence. The solicitor of these letters needs to spell out what kinds of evidence are sought. The call for specificity of data places the burden on the respondent. Exactly what does the letter say about the candidate? Is the evidence in the letter relevant to the criteria that are being used for promotion or tenure? Is the evidence first-hand, or is it based upon second- and third-hand information? These questions need to be raised whenever letters of support are used.

The chairman examines the evidence submitted by the candidate and tenured colleagues, and material in his own files as well as what might be in the central personnel file. These materials are synthesized into a letter of support or nonsupport. As a next step, some institutions include area committees or promotion and tenure committees that perform independent analyses of the evidence, using essentially the same materials as the chairman. The recommendation is passed on to the academic vice-president who usually makes a final recommendation to the president. Tenure decisions are generally reviewed by the president, who makes the final decision, and the board of trustees "passes" (rubber stamps) the list. Legally, however, the final decision rests with the board of trustees.

Of course this is only a model but most colleges and universities follow a similar pattern. And most of the patterns look quite logical on paper. But in practice their results are almost anti-intellectual. Some of the severe problems of the process are brought out in Hildebrand's example of a (fictitious) department chairman's letter of support. The letter describes what the candidate does, implying that these are good things to do. (Yet the research of Wilson and Hildebrand indicates that the best and worst teachers perform about the same academic activities.) The letter of support talks about classroom performance yet does not provide information about the sampling and evaluative procedures used to evaluate it. The support of colleagues in the department is mentioned but not the criteria by which these colleagues judged the individual. Hildebrand concludes that "adjectives such as outstanding and excellent have long since come into such wide use for summarizing teaching performance in promotion letters that the excesses of this chairman's last sentence ('Unquestionably he is an able, conscientious and worthy instructor') can be excused and ignored as in-house ritual, and experienced members of the review committee will do so" (1971, pp. 1–6).

Hildebrand's perceptive report illustrates some of the serious shortcomings in some procedures for promotion and tenure. Ironically, in making promotion and tenure decisions—those that have the greatest impact upon the future of the institution—the tendency is to use "seat-of-the-pants" criteria. Is it any wonder that state legislators, Ph.D. business executives, and even some professors are raising serious questions about internal management of colleges and universities?

FINAL WEIGHING

The key to a final weighing of selected criteria rests upon the three considerations mentioned earlier: the nature of the institution, the needs and directions of the department, and the interests and abilities of the individual. The "mix" of these three considerations amounts to a contract with the individual. Gaff and Wilson have written that "individualized contracts not only allow faculty to work on tasks in which they excel but also provide an explicit basis for an individualized evaluation. They can assure faculty that they will be evaluated on what they have explicitly agreed to do, rather than on some implicit generalized basis" (1970, p. 34).

Finally, the annual professional performance is calculated. This system makes two assumptions: the yearly professional responsibilities have been distributed in some way over the nine categories; the quantified instruments are used. The following five profiles are examples of how the system can be used for a variety of situations.

Professor A (Table 8) is a very busy person, spending his time on a wide variety of activities. He carries enough of an advis-

80

Determining Overall Performance Rating

Table 8.

Professor A	Percent of Total Effort		Criterion Rating		Raw Score
1. advising	10	×	6.3	=	63
2. teaching	50	×	6.1	=	305
3. faculty service	10	×	5.9	=	59
4. administration	—				
5. the arts	—				
6. professional status	10	×	4.9	=	49
7. publications	10	×	4.3	=	43
8. public service	10	×	4.9	=	49
9. research	—				
	100%				568

$$568 \div 700 = .81$$

ing load so that 10 per cent of his time is recognized for it, and his teaching responsibilities are 50 per cent of the full professional load. He is a member of an internal governance task force; he is chairman of the annual state convention in his discipline; he is struggling to finish a booklet; and he is serving on a major survey team appointed by the governor. (Few professors have, or would be able to cope with, a schedule like that of A, but there are a few.)

Professor B (Table 9) has quite a different pattern. He is primarily a teacher, with some advising responsibilities above the normal load. He also is chairman of the college's policy committee.

Professor C (Table 10) has no load-recognized responsibilities other than teaching.

Professor D (Table 11) is head of an eight-member department and this responsibility is given consideration in his professional workload. He also is at the critical stages of writing a textbook in

Table 9.

Professor B	Percent of Total Effort		Criterion Rating		Raw Score
1. advising	10	×	6.2	=	62
2. teaching	80	×	6.0	=	480
3. faculty service	10	×	5.7	=	57
4. administration	—				
5. the arts	—				
6. professional status	—				
7. publications	—				
8. public service	—				
9. research	—				
	100%				599

$$599 \div 700 = .86$$

Table 10.

Professor C	Percent of Total Effort		Criterion Rating		Raw Score
1. advising	—				
2. teaching	100	×	6.3	=	630
3. faculty service	—				
4. administration	—				
5. the arts	—				
6. professional status	—				
7. publications	—				
8. public service	—				
9. research	—				
	100%				630

$$630 \div 700 = .90$$

his discipline and this task is given significant weight for the academic year.

Professor E (Table 12) is in the theater department and a major segment of his responsibility calls for the production of two plays per academic year. In addition, he teaches a course on the theater and is writing the history of the theater in his state at the request of the state arts council.

Performance profile. The performance profile (see page 85) is the yearly summary of academic performance for one individual. The overall score on each activity is plotted, and the points are connected. No consideration is given to the weight given to each category. For example, the score on teaching would be plotted somewhere along the 1 to 7 continuum without consideration of the per cent of professional load represented by teaching.

Flexibility and individualization are the key concepts in the evaluation procedure suggested in this book. The system has considerable flexibility, and it can be tailored, insofar as institutional and departmental needs will allow, to individual interests and abilities. But is not the final "overall performance rating" too exact to have any general meaning and too mechanical to suit the art and complexities of academic life? Is it not demeaning to reduce professional performance to a percentage figure?

The system suggested in this book concludes with a percentage figure. Present evaluative procedures and institutional patterns do not allow one to say with certainty that a 90 per cent rating on overall performance is definitively better than an 88 per cent rating. But one can have some confidence that a 90 per cent rating is indicative of better performance than a score of 85 per cent; and the differences between 90 and 80 per cent ratings should tell something rather definite about overall performance. The extent to which it is demeaning to reduce overall professional performance to a percentage rating is a matter of opinion. Most professors still maintain a rather precise procedure for grading their students. When many personnel decisions in higher education are based upon fragmentary, subjective, and second-hand information—clearly erring on the side of imprecision—can serious objection be raised

Table 11.

Professor D	Percent of Total Effort		Criterion Rating		Raw Score
1. advising	—				
2. teaching	25	×	5.7	=	143
3. faculty service	—				
4. administration	25	×	6.2	=	155
5. the arts	—				
6. professional status	—				
7. publications	50	×	6.2	=	310
8. public service	—				
9. research					
	100%				608

$$608 \div 700 = .86$$

Table 12.

Professor E	Percent of Total Effort		Criterion Rating		Raw Score
1. advising	—				
2. teaching	25	×	5.7	=	143
3. faculty service	—				
4. administration	—				
5. the arts	50	×	5.9	=	295
6. professional status	—				
7. publications	25	×	5.7	=	143
8. public service	—				
9. research	—				
	100%				581

$$581 \div 700 = .83$$

84

PERFORMANCE PROFILE

For ....   Year ....

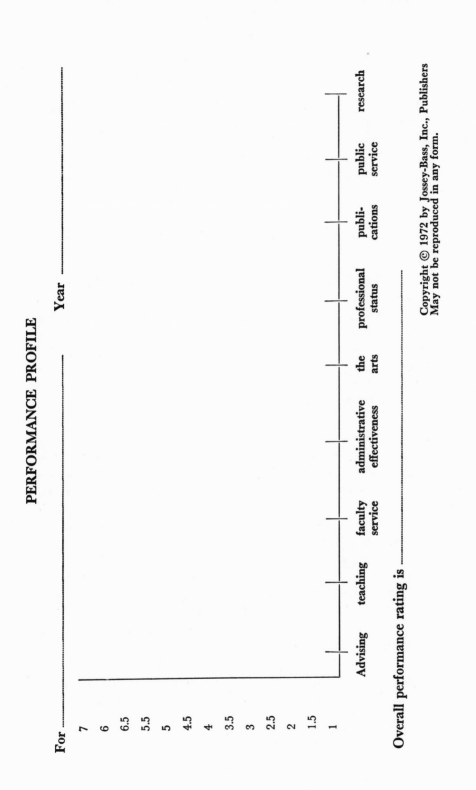

7							
6							
6.5							
5.5							
5							
4.5							
4							
3.5							
3							
2.5							
2							
1.5							
1							

Advising   teaching   faculty service   administrative effectiveness   the arts   professional status   publi-cations   public service   research

Overall performance rating is ....

against a system that attempts to bring a greater degree of sensitivity, fairness, and precision into the overall process?

Are there aspects of this system which can be useful to those institutions which, for one reason or another, cannot implement it in its entirety? College X is a teaching institution, and its survival depends upon its success in this area. Teaching is primary in every faculty member's professional load and no load credit is given for advising, faculty service, professional status, publications, public service, or research. Each of these activities must be performed in addition to the full teaching load. Given even these circumstances, the institution can still use the system in two basic ways. Use only the teaching category (even this will be an advancement for some institutions). Assign a figure of something less than 100 per cent for classroom teaching even though the individual has a full teaching load. The difference between 100 and the figure assigned, say 75, can be used for other categories. This procedure is consistent with the fact that one's professional activities do tally up to 100 per cent whether forty or seventy hours are spent on them.

IN CONCLUSION

Heisenberg, one of the early leaders in theoretical atomic physics, developed the principle of indeterminacy, or the "uncertainty principle," which states that the position and velocity of an electron in motion cannot be measured simultaneously with high precision. The Heisenberg principle is accepted by scientists as honest recognition of imprecision yet it has in no way deterred the relentless pursuit of precision. Something of this spirit is necessary with respect to the system of evaluation outlined in this book. It has its imprecisions, uncertainties, and threatening aspects; yet it is backed by an impressive backlog of research and expert opinion, demands for better performances, and the need to know more about the teaching/learning process.

In the final analysis, only people can make systems, programs, or organizations work. The process of developing, introducing, and managing a system of evaluation is a human problem.

Determining Overall Performance Rating

The sensitivities and fears of individuals are real and need always to be considered in the implementation of any system, but a progressive and dynamic college or university is built by accentuating the positive and by moving ahead.

Appendix *A* ☙☙☙☙☙☙☙

Computer Experience
with Student Evaluation
(North Carolina State)

☙☙☙☙☙☙☙☙☙☙

*W*hat costs can be expected when a college or university under-takes a campus-wide computerized program of faculty evaluation? Four years of cost data are presented through the courtesy of North Carolina State University.

Year	Supplies	Salaries	Computer	Annual Total
1967–68	$1420	$ 835	$2535	$4790
1968–69	925	655	2520	4100
1969–70	545	500	2540	3585
1970–71	1255	2060* (460)	4000	7315 (5715)

* Computer programing salary costs included for the first time.
Previously no amount had been calculated for this cost.

89

Evaluating Faculty Performance

The North Carolina experience with the computerized process of faculty evaluation is described by Clauston Jenkins, coordinator of institutional studies and planning:

> There are four major aspects of the process: logistics; changes; interpretation; and cost. To start with logistics, I should point out that computerization demands accuracy; thus, handling of materials cannot be done haphazardly. In addition, computerization means that there are more steps in the evaluation process and thus more chances for errors. In my judgment, computerization of faculty evaluation simplifies the tabulation of results but does not simplify or reduce the work involved in obtaining the raw data.
>
> Second, changes in the evaluation and changes in computer center staff have great impact. Changes in the evaluation can require major revisions in the computer programs. When programs are changed it is easy for errors to occur, but one often does not know about the error until the computer has printed out some nonsense which has been distributed. For example, because of a slight program change the computer program that calculates departmental averages did not work properly and printed the same average for each question for every department. Changes in computer center staff mean that new programmers have to learn what is going on, and this process can be costly in time and mistakes. Computer programmers vary greatly in ability and they tend to change jobs even more often than faculty did in the good old days.
>
> Third, once the data is on the computer and the results have been run, there is a need for interpretation. Our computer program prints out a series of numerical averages and faculty find it difficult at times to translate these numbers into improvement in their teaching. We have tried to help some by providing departmental and university wide averages but we need to and could do much more provided we had the resources.
>
> Finally, use of computerized evaluation is far more costly in terms of real time and computer time. As a result there are limits to what we can do with the data we have accumulated and these limitations are a source of frustration to the administration and faculty. As the financial squeeze hits us harder (and it is hitting us), we may have to reduce the scope of the present process.

90

Computer Experience with Student Evaluation

Even with the problems mentioned above, and I have emphasized the negative aspects in order to illustrate that the computer is no panacea, we feel that our computerized evaluation is working and is being used. Faculty use the results to select outstanding teachers. Department heads use the results in considering promotions and merit increases; some school deans use the results in determining the effectiveness of their curricula; and the Provost uses the results in reviewing promotions and salary increases. Like any process of evaluation it meets resistance. We now have a standing university committee established to review the whole issue of teacher effectiveness so who knows what changes are in the offing?

Appendix B

Analysis of Student Appraisal of Instruction Form

The initial form for student appraisal of instruction was developed at the University of Kentucky. Extensive changes were made, based upon eighteen months of trial, modification, and further trials at the University of Kentucky. Many additional changes were made as a result of detailed analysis by the liaison committee of Baldwin-Wallace College.

A special Baldwin-Wallace task force on instruction and development was appointed by the academic dean in March 1970. For almost one year, the committee met and developed an overall plan, including extensive research on the student appraisal of instruction form. On April 27 and 28, 1970, the student appraisal form and a student self-evaluation form were administered by some of the teaching faculty to some of the students. On May 29 and June 1 and 2, 1970, the student appraisal of instruction form was administered by the faculty to the student body.[1] A maximum of 2750 completed forms produced the data for the research.[2]

[1] The basic research was done by S. Lee Whiteman, associate professor of psychology, Baldwin-Wallace College.
[2] The research was done on the student appraisal form at a time

92

Analysis of Student Appraisal of Instruction Form

1. The product moment correlation between the first test and the second test was +.68, with significance at the .01 level, indicating that the evaluation form has fairly good test-retest reliability. The overall rating score for professors by students was 59.20 on the first test and 61.43 on the second one. The 2.23 improvement may be an instructional improvement, although a cause-and-effect relationship cannot be established.

A high correlation between first and second administrations is not necessarily desirable if little change toward improvement in mean ratings has not taken place. The main reason for giving the first test early in the quarter is to spot weaknesses that might be eliminated over the quarter.

2. On the second test, each item was correlated with the total score on the appraisal form, with these results.[3]

A. Considering the previous fourteen items, how would you rate this professor in comparison to all others you have had?　　$r = +.81$

B. How would you describe the attitude of fellow classmates toward your professor?　　$r = +.72$

C. Have the major objectives of the course been made clear?　　$r = +.68$

D. Are important ideas clearly explained?　　$r = +.68$

E. Is class time well used?　　$r = +.68$

F. How do you rate agreement between course objectives and lesson assignments?　　$r = +.67$

G. How well are class presentations planned and organized?　　$r = +.67$

---

when the scale was from 5 (highest) to 1 (lowest). Subsequently, the scale was changed to 7 (highest) and 1 (lowest). This change is not judged to influence the basic findings of the five-point scale.

[3] All correlations are significant at the .01 level of significance.

H. Has the professor encouraged critical thinking and analysis? $r = +.66$

I. Do you believe the professor encouraged relevant student involvement in the class? $r = +.60$

J. Did your professor encourage you to seek his help when necessary? $r = +.59$

K. Are you being graded fairly in this class? $r = +.58$

L. How does the professor react to viewpoints different from his own? $r = +.56$

M. How would you judge the professor's mastery of the course content? $r = +.54$

N. Does your professor have speaking mannerisms or personal traits that interfere with learning? $r = +.47$

O. How much time and effort did you put into the class compared to classes of equal credit? $r = +.45$

From this analysis, items N and O were dropped from the subsequent revision of the form, which took place in the fall of 1970.

3. An analysis of the two administrations of the appraisal form as well as a self-evaluation form filled in by the students, resulted in these findings:

A. No significant relationship between the student's reported grade point average and his ratings on the form was found.

$(r = +.01/$not significant at .01 level$)$

B. No significant relationship between the student's anticipated grade in a course and his ratings on the form was found.

$(r = +.05/$not significant at .01 level$)$

Analysis of Student Appraisal of Instruction Form

C. Students in small classes tend to rate professors higher than students in large classes.

(t = 3.20/significant at .01 level)

D. Students in upper division classes tend to rate professors higher than students in lower division classes.

(t = 3.02/significant at .01 level)

E. No significant difference between students who took a course because it was required and those who took the course because they desired to do so was found.

(t = .82/not significant)

F. No significant difference in ratings by students who said the course fitted well into schedule and those who said that it did not was found.

(t = 1.31/not significant)

G. Students who heard the professor was good rated him higher than those who heard otherwise.

(t = 9.40/significant at .01 level)

H. Students who had a genuine interest in the subject matter rated the professor higher than those who expressed little interest.

(t = 6.44/significant at .01 level)

I. Students who prepared assignments daily rated the professor higher than those who reported that they did not.

(t = 4.58/significant at .01 level)

J. Those who did considerable independent work out of class rated the professor higher than those who said that they did not.

(t = 4.77/significant at .01 level)

K. Those who answered "yes" when asked whether they did anything at all for the course rated the professor no differently from those who reported "no."

(t = 1.16/not significant)

L. Those who said that too much work was demanded of them in the course rated the professor higher than those who felt the course demands to be negligible or just right.

$$(F = 3.23/\text{significant at .05 level})$$

M. Those who frequently voluntarily participated in class rated the professor higher than those who volunteered occasionally or never.

$$(F = 15.17/\text{significant at .01 level})$$

N. Those who sought out explanations for materials not understood rated the professor higher than those who did not.

$$(t = 5.66/\text{significant at .01 level})$$

O. Those who looked up minor points not understood in class rated the professor higher than those who did not.

$$(t = 5.24/\text{significant at .01 level})$$

P. Those who monopolized class discussions rated the professor higher than those who did not.

$$(t = 2.02/\text{significant at the .05 level})$$

Q. Those who made relationships between new and old material rated the professor higher than those who did not.

$$(t = 4.68/\text{significant at .01 level})$$

R. Those who made relationships between the course and other courses rated the professor higher than those who did not.

$$(t = 4.23/\text{significant at. 01 level})$$

S. Those who were getting as much as anticipated from the course rated the professor higher than those who were not.

$$(t = 12.93/\text{significant at .01 level})$$

Selected and Annotated Bibliography

$\mathcal{T}$ he following entries date from 1960 and include a variety of materials on various aspects of faculty evaluation. This bibliography is based upon one prepared by Terry Leigh.

The few entries not annotated are referenced in the text but, as total works, do not necessarily focus on faculty evaluation.

American Academy of Arts and Sciences, Assembly on University Goals and Governance. *A First Report*. Cambridge, Mass., 1971.

American Educational Research Association. *Handbook of Research on Teaching*. Chicago: Rand McNally, 1963.

ANDERSON, C. C., AND HUNKA, S. M. "Teacher Evaluation: Some Problems and a Proposal." *Harvard Educational Review*, 1963, *33*, 74–95.

Pupils, evaluators, and administrators consider quite different attributes in conceptualizing the competent teacher. A step toward better understanding of the problems relating to teacher competency may be the intensive and extensive study of teacher characteristics. Some of these may be spontaneity, initiative, voluntary social contributions, acts of problem solving, and significantly fewer attributes such as conflict with others and boredom.

ANDERSON, R. C., AND OTHERS. *Current Research on Instruction.* Englewood Cliffs, N.J.: Prentice-Hall, 1969. 396 pp.

The book is intended as a text or supplementary source for students of education and students of psychology concerned with its application to education. The main themes are: approaches to instructional research and development, instructional objectives, prompting and fading techniques, the student response, reinforcement and feedback, facilitation of concept learning, organization and sequence, and evaluation of instruction. The articles in sections devoted to the above themes are taken from a variety of sources.

AUSTIN, A. W., AND LEE, C. B. T. "Current Practices in the Evaluation and Training of College Teachers." *The Educational Record*, 1966, *47*, 361–365.

The purpose of the survey of 1110 institutions was to provide an empirical basis for a critical appraisal of current practices and to determine a point of departure from which proposals for improving existing techniques could be developed.

The most frequently used of fifteen sources of information for determining teaching effectiveness are: evaluations by department chairman (85% responded use in all or most departments); evaluations by the dean (82%); the opinions of colleagues (49%); scholarly research and publications (44%); and informal student opinions (41%). Classroom visits are used very infrequently (taboo at 40% of the institutions); evaluations often are based on hearsay evidence (informal student opinions). The data clearly indicate that research and publication are the primary considerations in evaluating teaching ability.

Criteria considered by all institutions as major factors for salary increase, promotion, and tenure were: classroom teaching (96%); personal attributes (57%); length of service in rank (47%); research (47%). At universities, research is almost equal in consideration to teaching. More selective and affluent colleges and larger institutions are more likely to use research and publication as criteria.

BAYLEY, D. H. "Making College Teaching a Profession." *Improving College and University Teaching,* 1967, *15,* 115–19.

Most college teachers believe that they are fully capable of criticizing their own teaching performance. However, the present system indicates that such evaluations can hardly be accepted at face value. The author sees two alternatives— students and other observers. Since, by and large, teachers reject student evaluations, their worth may be judged by setting them alongside qualified observers—other college teachers. Colleague evaluation will provide trustworthy criticism, an essential element of feedback—agreement as to teaching performance—and information for rewarding and punishing teachers.

BELKNAP, E. H., AND OTHERS. "Guidelines for Promotion." *Improving College and University Teaching,* 1965, *13,* 14–15.

Recommendations by the Division of Education Personnel Committee at San Fernando State College on policies to be followed in relation to hiring, orientation, and promotion of staff members were based on the assumption that faculty promotions are made on the basis of personal judgments. These judgments, then, must be distilled from the largest source of information available to the judges sought from all those who are in a position to know. Information was grouped into three areas: good teaching at the college level; contribution to division and college; and professional growth.

99

BIRNBAUM, R. "Background and Evaluation of Faculty in New York." *The Junior College Journal,* 1966, *38,* 34–37.

Twenty-seven of the thirty-four public, two-year colleges in New York State were surveyed on twelve factors as criteria for promotion and tenure. The two top-ranked factors were teaching performance and effectiveness, and academic preparation and continuing education. Last-ranked factors were community service, and scholarly research and publications, respectively.

BLACKMAN, A. F., AND OTHERS. "Students Rate Their Professors and Courses." *Phi Delta Kappan,* 1967, *48,* 266–269.

The authors undertook the production of a booklet in which professors and students would discuss their courses. Student opinion was solicited by questionnaire, and a summary of the course was written. The professor was then forwarded the summary and invited to reply. The professor's reply was printed along with the summary in the booklet. The objectives were: to inform students about their prospective courses; to provide professors with feedback about their teaching; and to influence academic policy or effect changes in the teaching of courses. Eighty per cent of professors replied to the summaries. A 30 per cent student response was needed for a summary to be written.

BOGUE, E. G. "Student Appraisal of Teaching Effectiveness in Higher Education; Summary of the Literature." *Educational Quest,* 1967, *11,* 6–10.

There has been a lack of scientific basis for the educational practice of evaluation. The article presents various opinions on the need for utilization of student opinions in the evaluative process. Evaluation does not eliminate the need for value judgment.

Selected and Annotated Bibliography

BOURGEOIS, D. P. "A Study of Faculty Opinion Concerning Selected Factors Related to Excellence in Teaching at the University of Southwestern Louisiana." Unpublished M. A. thesis. University of Southwestern Louisiana, 1967.

The purpose of the project was to solicit faculty opinion as to undergraduate program accreditation, benefits derived from educational courses that deal with teacher preparation, promotion policy, and views of the faculty concerning student evaluation. An examination of the literature pertaining to the study indicated that: (1) the Ph.D. does not indicate that a good teacher is produced; (2) the Ph.D. prepares the recipient as a researcher and not a teacher; (3) only one-half of all that earn a doctorate find their way into teaching; (4) the present graduate colleges train researchers and not teachers; (5) only ten per cent of the faculty accounts for ninety per cent of the research and publication in any university; and (6) in any given year, no more than thirty per cent of an average university faculty will be engaged in research.

Analysis of questionnaires indicated that there was a lack of qualified faculty members if the proper credential for college teaching is the doctorate. A small percentage of the faculty members had the prescribed professional educational courses required for good college teaching. Many faculty statements indicate that the faculty was unfamiliar with the policy for promotions at the university. The faculty perceived the students as having some ability to evaluate excellence in teaching, and some benefits could accrue from observation of such a practice.

BROUDY, H. S. "Can We Define Good Teaching?" *The Teachers College Record*, 1969, *70*, 583–592.

Good teaching can be defined well enough for experts to use in evaluation, but chances of reaching agreement are far greater in didactic than in encounter teaching. The machine is the norm for didactic efficiency; the humanely cultivated person is the model for the latter. However, there is an endless variation of this model, and the problem for the schools is to lure enough teachers to do the necessary encounter teaching, a task that is more important than defining our preferred variety of it.

BROWN, D. W. "Teach Or Perish." *Improving College and University Teaching,* 1967, *15,* 108–110.

The "five C's" of evaluation require that the enterprise be cooperative, comprehensive, constructive, clinical, and continuous. Colleague evaluation should constitute 60 to 75 per cent of the final decision. A realistic system of rewards must be provided. Competent analytical study should determine judgment, and evaluation should be thorough and continuous.

BRYAN, R. C., "Student Rating of Teachers," *Improving College and University Teaching,* 1968, *16,* 200–202.

A 1966–67 survey investigated student-initiated appraisal of teaching. Of the 307 institutions that reported, 149 (49 per cent) had a plan for student appraisal of teaching; 117 (38 per cent) had never systematically obtained student ratings of teachers; and 41 (13 per cent) had discontinued student ratings after a trial period. Other follow-up questions were sent to the responding institutions.

BRYANT, P. T. "By Their Fruits Ye Shall Know Them." *The Journal of Higher Education,* 1967, *38,* 326–330.

University administrators agree that effective teaching, not research, should head the list of considerations for rewards. Three methods for recognizing and rewarding good teaching are discussed. Student evaluation is considered invalid by the author due to their immaturity, elective versus required courses, and class size. Administrative evaluation could be worthwhile, yet is seldom conducted. Peer evaluation is best conducted by a department chairman or his delegate through visitation, discussion, and examination of course materials and examinations.

BYRNES, F. C., AND JAMRICH, J. X. "Survey of Policies and Practices Relating to Improved Instruction." *Improvement of Instruction in Higher Education.* Report to The American Association of Colleges for Teacher Education, 1962.

The survey was designed to elicit information from each member institution about policies and practices relating to instruction. Analysis of the 310 questionnaires returned indicated that promotion and salary increases are the two reward practices most frequently mentioned. Outstanding teaching alone serves as a basis for promotion in rank in 52% of the institutions, while 87% indicate salary increases are made on this basis. The appraisal and evaluation technique used by 63 per cent in assessing teaching ability for promotion or salary increases is information gathered via "the grapevine." Administration observance is reported by 46 per cent, with this being least characteristic of universities with enrollments exceeding 25,000. Eighty-eight per cent, however, indicate that the administrators evaluate teaching for purposes of salary increases and promotion. Peer group appraisal, student achievement, and student rating systems were also discussed.

COHEN, S. "Evaluation of Teachers." *Journal of Dental Education,* 1967, *30,* 225–228.

Teachers are presently evaluated for two main purposes— recruitment and promotion. Recruitment factors usually have little bearing on teaching competence and promotion often depends upon how well the candidate is liked. Deans and department heads are generally responsible for evaluation. Student results have been surprisingly good. Priority has been placed on the ability to do research. Future suggestions may include classifying teachers into categories such as seminar leader, lecturer-teacher, clinical teacher, laboratory teacher, and so forth. Benefits of objective teacher evaluation include teacher recognition, enhancement of student learning, and security for teacher and student.

COOK, J. M., AND NEVILLE, R. F. *The Faculty as Teachers: A Perspective on Evaluation,* Report 13. Washington, D.C.: ERIC Clearinghouse on Higher Education, One Dupont Circle, 1971. 14 pp.

Evaluation methods currently in use are reviewed and a recommendation for the implementation of an approach is made. Teaching effectiveness is defined as the study of teaching outcomes. The authors analyze the relative merits of measurement based on student performance (direct measurement) and measurement based on teaching activities (indirect measurement).

CORTEZ, J. D. *The Design and Validation of an Evaluative Instrument To Appraise the Teaching Effectiveness of the College Instructor.* Doctoral dissertation. University of Denver, 1967. 153 pages. (Dissertation Abstracts, Volume 28, Number 2435-A, 1967).

The study was conducted in three general phases: the design of the evaluative instrument; a pilot study of the evaluative procedure to test its operational feasibility; and the implementation of the evaluative procedure in seven colleges and universities in Colorado. It was concluded that the Professional Competence Guide was a practical instrument for evaluating teaching effectiveness and professional competence.

Selected and Annotated Bibliography

Cox Commission. *Crisis at Columbia.* New York: Random House, 1968.

DAUGHERTY, H. A., "Appraising College Teachers," *Improving College and University Teaching,* 1968, *16,* 203–206.

> While there is universal agreement that evaluation at the college level is necessary and desirable, several knotty problems immediately arise to give a sobering and meditative slant to this consideration: should research ability or scholarly productivity be evaluated; how and on what bases is evaluation made; what are the measurable objectives; who should make the evaluation; and what use is made of evaluation? The article addresses itself to these questions, quoting from various authors and studies.

DE BRIUM, H. C. "Quality Instruction." *Improving College and University Teaching,* 1967, *15,* 214–215.

> Explains a rating instrument developed in an attempt to isolate certain characteristics of good teaching. It was hypothesized that these characteristics are in the realm of self-concept and personality. Graduate students were asked to rate the instructors' overall ability and then check any one of the ten factors under the "observed instructor self-concept" that they felt were evident.

DENNIS, L. E., AND JACOB, R. M. (Eds.). *The Arts in Higher Education.* San Francisco: Jossey-Bass, 1968.

DRESSEL, P. L. "Teaching, Learning and Evaluation." In H. A. Estrin and D. M. Goode (Eds.), *College and University Teaching.* Dubuque, Iowa: William Brown Company, 1964.

> Evaluation is inseparable from instruction in learning, and the implicit and explicit objectives should coincide to allow for meaningful objectives. Rational determination of objectives requires consideration of change in amount and direc-

tion. Evaluation all too often emphasizes errors and ignores strengths. Instruction requires providing opportunities for the student to practice behavior stated in faculty objectives. Students should recognize shared responsibility for effectiveness, and evaluation should be learned experience for both teacher and student.

DRESSEL, P. L. "Evaluation of Instruction." *Journal of Farm Economics,* 1967, *49,* 299.

Student ratings have been found to be fairly consistent, regardless of grade or class level. Yet, due to the instructor's displeasure with the process, it may be more realistic to have the students engage in a broader type of evaluation in reference to the course or the total learning experience. Observation by peers or by administrative superiors is regularly practiced by some institutions and probably should be more common. The prevailing tradition of academic freedom has made it difficult to initiate methods such as classroom recordings and similar devices. Good instruction depends upon curriculum organization and the facilities available, upon objectives, methods, and materials, and upon how these are organized and interrelated.

DRESSEL, P. L. "Faculty Development, Appraisal, and Reward." Unpublished document. Michigan State University, n.d.

The report covers six major areas of faculty activity: professional competence and professional activity (scholarship and advanced study, research, professional activity); curriculum planning and evaluation; classroom teaching (planning of instruction, evaluation, effective communication, evaluation of teaching); academic advising of students; public service; and faculty statesmanship. Faculty evaluation is not merely a matter of looking at instruction or research; faculty development involves a determination of what each person can do best and the utilization of these talents.

Selected and Annotated Bibliography

DRESSEL, P. L., AND ASSOCIATES. *Evaluation in Higher Education.* Boston: Houghton Mifflin, 1961. 480 pp.

> The thirteen chapters are written by various authorities, and follow this pattern: chapters 1–3 consider successively the nature and role of evaluation, the significance and the problems of defining educational objectives, and the relationship of evaluation to the learning process; chapters 4–7 treat specific evaluation and testing problems in the four broad areas of social science, the natural sciences, the humanities, and communications. Chapters 8 and 9 are closely related to the previous four chapters; and chapters 10–13 consider the nature and role of evaluation in several phases of institutional planning and policy determination.

DRESSEL, P. L., JOHNSON, F. C., AND MARCUS, P. M. *The Confidence Crisis: An Analysis of University Departments.* San Francisco: Jossey-Bass, 1970.

EBLE, K. E. "Project to Improve College Teaching," *Academe,* 1970, *4,* 3–6.

> This special section of the AAUP publication describes a two-year study jointly sponsored by the AAUP and the Association of American Colleges. It was designed as a career development study and begins with methods for attracting talented persons into the profession, follows their development as college teachers, and concludes with a consideration of how to maintain teaching effectiveness throughout a faculty member's career. "Evaluation" is the major topic.

EBLE, K. E. *Professors as Teachers.* San Francisco, Jossey-Bass, 1972.

> This small book is an essential work for those interested in this field. Its contents include: recognition of teaching, evaluation and the improvement of teaching, student eval-

107

uation instruments and procedures, impact of student evaluation and faculty review. A bibliography is included.

Faculty Advisory Committee of the President and Board of Trustees. "Staff Specialization: The Unexploited Key to the Development of the Full Potential of Each Professor and Department of the Modern University. (Mimeograph) Ohio State University, 1967.

FISHMAN, J. "Cross-Cultural Perspective on the Evaluation of Guided Behavioral Change." *The Evaluation of Teaching.* Washington, D.C.: Pi Lambda Theta, 1967, 9–31.

The evaluation of teaching effectiveness in the United States has concentrated on teacher characteristics and behavior. While it is clear that teacher and method are important to the learning process, we cannot yet say just what it is that the effective teacher is or does. Teaching cannot be evaluated independently of learning, nor can learning be evaluated independently of teaching. American teachers must learn to accept evaluation.

GAFF, J. G., WILSON, R. C., AND OTHERS. *The Teaching Environment: A Study of Optimum Working Conditions for Effective College Teaching.* Berkeley, Calif.: Center for Research and Development in Higher Education, 1970, 63 pp.

The report includes several sections that bear directly on faculty performance and evaluation: views of teachers, institutional supports for good teaching, relationships with students, relationships with colleagues, reward structure, teaching evaluation, and work load. The authors conclude that: (1) faculty members should be aware of general developments in higher education, especially those developments most directly related to teaching and learning; (2) there should be a visible comprehensive program to assist the personal and professional development of faculty members; (3) there should be provision for faculty members to obtain useful feedback from students concerning their teaching activities; (4) there should be periodic reviews of the instructional program and proposals for its improvement; (5) intelligent efforts to restructure curricula and reform courses are valuable but probably insufficient.

GAGE, N. L. "Ends and Means in Appraising College Teaching." In W. J. McKeachie (Ed.), *The Appraisal of Teaching in Large Universities*. Ann Arbor, Michigan: University of Michigan, 1959.

GAGE, N. L. "The Appraisal of College Teaching." *Journal of Higher Education*, 1961, *32*, 17–22.

Appraisals must be fair; teachers should not be penalized for conditions over which they have no control, such as the level of the course, the size of the class, whether the course is elective or required, and where it is taught. Research conducted at the University of Illinois indicated that: (1) teachers of lower level courses had lower ratings than did those of more advanced courses; (2) teachers with a class load of thirty to thirty-nine students had lower ratings than did instructors with fewer students; (3) instructors and assistant professors received lower ratings than did associate professors and professors; (4) off-campus instructors received higher ratings than on-campus instructors, and (5) teachers of elective courses had higher ratings than did instructors of required courses.

GARDNER, J. W. "Agenda for Colleges and Universities." In A. C. Eurich (Ed.), *Campus 1980*. New York: Dell Publishing, 1968.

GOODE, D. M. *72 College Teaching Procedures*. Corvallis, Oregon: Oregon State University Press, 1966.

Briefly describes seventy-two procedures for increasing the

effectiveness of college teaching. These procedures strengthen teacher competence and therefore provide the instructor with better ratings on evaluation.

GOODE, D. M. "Evaluation and Teaching." *Journal of Dental Education,* 1967, *30,* 260–264.

Emphasizes that a profession, such as dentistry, can exist only if it rests on a theory or technology. Evaluation is an ongoing process of identifying and defining values. Visitation, testing procedures, and appraisal by students should be utilized in evaluative techniques.

GRAY, C. E., "The Teaching Model and Evaluation of Teaching Performance," *Journal of Higher Education,* 1969, *40,* 636–642.

A model of the skills and strategies involved in teaching is given. Teacher behavior is thought of as linguistic, performative, and expressive. The article also presents a model for evaluating certain observable aspects of classroom teaching.

GUILD, R. "Criterion Problem in Instructor Evaluation." *Journal of Dental Education,* 1967, *30,* 270–279.

The article takes the position that the need common to measurement is for a criterion with which the to-be-measured phenomenon can be compared. Criteria that could be used for the evaluation of dental instructors could be formulated under the headings of code of instructional ethics; position description: significant working relations with others, specific work, job knowledge, technical knowledge of teaching and learning; student opinion; and student achievement.

GUSTAD, J. W. *Policies and Practices in Faculty Evaluation.* Washington, D.C.: Committee on College Teaching, American Council on Education, 1961. 18 pp.

Evaluation practices were studied in 584 institutions. In the large majority of cases, those principally responsible for evaluation were the president, the dean, and the department (or division) chairman. Of the factors considered in making evaluations, all seven types of institutions said that classroom teaching was the most important. Other factors mentioned in order of frequency were: personal attributes, student advising, research, publication, committee work, professional society activity, length of service in rank, public service, supervision of graduate study, consultation, competing offers, and supervision of honors.

Six sources of data most frequently used for evaluating classroom teaching were: informal student opinion; formal student opinion (student ratings); classroom visitation; colleagues' opinions; and the opinions of chairmen and deans.

The faculty resume was the most frequently mentioned source for evaluating research and publications; other frequently mentioned sources were the opinions of colleagues, chairmen, and deans. At least one-half of the institutions stated that they were dissatisfied with their present evaluation policies.

GUSTAD, J. W. "Evaluation of Teaching Performance: Issues and Possibilities." In C. B. T. Lee (Ed.), *Improving College Teaching*. Washington, D.C.: American Council on Education, 1967, pp. 265–281.

The report lists major trends abstracted from a comparative analysis of the 1961 and 1966 surveys conducted by the American Council on Education. These trends indicate: decline in the use of systematic student ratings; decline in classroom visitation; greater utilization of committee evaluation; greater analysis of grade distributions; wide use of informal student opinions, and evaluation by deans and chairmen; and almost total absence of research on the validity of the instruments used.

111

HAMMOND, P. E., AND OTHERS. "Teaching versus Research: Sources of Misperceptions," *The Journal of Higher Education*, 1969, *40*:682–690.

What is the relationship between teaching and research? The authors explore a number of structural features in academic communities which promote inaccurate perceptions. The central functions of these communities—teaching and research—are misperceived because of the segmentation of academic communities, leaving each person to form opinions largely from the perspective of his own structural position.

HARDEE, M. D. *The Faculty in College Counseling.* New York: McGraw-Hill, 1959.

HARVEY, J. N., AND BARKER, D. G. "Student Evaluation of Teaching Effectiveness," *Improving College and University Teaching*, 1970, *18*, 275–278.

The relationship between students' gross subjective judgments and their responses to a typical rating scale are examined. The basic data were collected from 118 male students. The ten items rated highest on a scale of 21 were: objectives clarified by the instructor, organization of course, knowledge of subject, range of interests and culture, preparation for class, skill as lecturer, skill as discussion leader, variety in classroom techniques, assignments, and ability to arouse interest.

HATCH, W. R., AND BENNET, A. "Effectiveness in Teaching." *New Dimensions in Higher Education*. Washington: U.S. Department of Health, Education, and Welfare, 1965, *2*. 28 pp.

Studies in various areas of teacher effectiveness are outlined. New research on the effectiveness of teaching suggests: that class size is not the critical factor but rather the nature of teaching as it affects learning; that one method is no more effective than another; and that problem-oriented approaches are becoming more effective.

HEXTER, J. H. "Publish or Perish—a Defense." *The Public Interest,* 1969, *17,* 60–77.

The writer develops the argument for the "publish or perish" position, using the widely publicized Yale incident as the focal point. "The advantage of Publish or Perish is that it breaks through two parochial and absurd assumptions: (1) that all university teaching goes on in the classroom, and (2) that in all teaching that goes on there is a pure act of creation on the part of the classroom teacher."

HIGHET, G. *The Art of Teaching.* New York: Alfred A. Knopf, 1950.

HILDEBRAND, M. "How to Recommend Promotion for a Mediocre Teacher Without Actually Lying." *Experiment and Innovation: New Directions in Education at the University of California.* 1971, *4,* 1–21.

This is a narrative report of a "hypothetical" case involving the promotion of Dr. Blank. The author clinically analyzes the letters of recommendation and concludes that they are quite inadequate. An unfortunate consequence to the promotion of mediocre teachers is that in the process some excellent teachers are denied promotion. The article also analyzes twenty-three objections of those who oppose the regular use of student evaluation of teaching. Some research findings from the University of California at Davis study of student evaluation of instruction are also included.

HILDEBRAND, M., AND WILSON, R. C. *Effective University Teaching and Its Evaluation.* Berkeley, Calif.: Center for Research and Development in Higher Education, 1970. 28 pp.

113

Evaluating Faculty Performance

The objective of the study conducted at the University of California at Davis was to contribute to the improvement of university teaching by characterizing effective performance and providing a satisfactory basis for the evaluation of teaching. The principal results: (1) there is excellent agreement among students, and between faculty and students, about the effectiveness of given teachers; (2) best and worst teachers engage in the same professional activities and allocate their time among academic pursuits in about the same ways; (3) analysis of eighty-five items characterizing best teachers as perceived by students produced five components of effective performance—analytic/synthetic approach, organization/clarity, instructor-group interaction, instructor-individual student interaction, and dynamism/enthusiasm; (4) analysis of the items characterizing best teachers as perceived by colleagues produced these five components of effective performance—research activity and recognition, intellectual breadth, participation in the academic community, relations with students, and concern for teaching.

HILGERT, R. L. "Teacher or Researcher?" *The Educational Forum,* 1964, *28,* 463–468.

Those who insist that a professor's first interest should be teaching argue the following points: (1) degree, research, or publication do not guarantee that one will be an effective teacher; (2) knowledge of the subject is secondary to the ability to impart knowledge to the student; and (3) promotions and salary increases should be based first of all on the professor's competence as a teacher.

Those who favor research and writing offer the following points: (1) research and writing reinforce the teaching efforts; (2) students consider the professor's knowledge to be authoritative when he has published a substantial amount;

114

(3) research and writing are modes of preparation for classroom presentation; (4) research updates teaching; and (5) professors should speak out in today's troubled world. The answer to the problem remains a matter of individual choice.

HODGKINSON, H. L. *Faculty Reward and Assessment Systems.* Unpublished manuscript. Berkeley, Calif.: Center for Research and Development in Higher Education, n.d.

Any system which attempts to assess and reward "competence" in teaching should be highly flexible and individualistic. Classroom evaluation is less than professional unless other professionals are in the room watching the teacher teach. Any legitimate system of faculty assessment should not only measure the faculty member in terms of where he is but what his growth patterns are.

HOLMES, D. S., *The Effects of Disconfirmed Grade Expectancies on Students' Evaluations of Their Instructor: A Study of Attitude Change.* Unpublished document. Princeton, N.J.: Educational Testing Service, 1970. 10 pp.

Half the students who deserved and expected A's and B's were given their expected grades while half were given a grade that was one step lower than they had expected. After receiving their grades, the students (University of Texas) filled out the teaching assessment form used there. A two-by-two analysis of variance revealed no differences in evaluations as a function of differences in grades, but evaluations on eleven of the nineteen items were lowered as a function of the unexpected lowering of grades. It was concluded that although differences in actual grades do not affect evaluations, if students' grades disconfirm their expectancies, the students will tend to depreciate the instructor's performance in areas other than his grading system.

HOLMES, D. S. "The Teaching Assessment Blank: A Form for the

115

Student Assessment of College Instructors," *The Journal of Experimental Education,* 1971, *39,* 34–38.

A factor analysis based on evaluations filled out by 1648 students at the University of Texas revealed four factors which measured the quality of the instructors' presentations, the evaluation process and the student-instructor interactions, the degree to which the students were stimulated and motivated by the instructors, and the clarity of the tests. A further analysis indicated that subscale scores reflecting the factor scores could be developed from the total item pool.

HOWE, H. "Less Teaching, More Conversation." In C. B. T. Lee (Ed.), *Improving College Teaching.* Washington, D.C.: American Council on Education, 1967.

HUMPHREY, D. C., AND MC CREARY, E. C. "Evaluating the Teaching of History." *Liberal Education,* 1970, *56,* 519–531.

A survey of more than one hundred history departments found that many colleges either ignored evaluation or found it an insurmountable task. Based upon this finding, the authors (in the history department at Carnegie-Mellon University) developed a system of evaluation for history. Their statement of "criteria for good teaching" consists of two parts: a discussion of criteria for substantive goals in history courses, and a discussion of four important conditions of learning (motivation, high standards of performance, structure, and guidance). The essay concludes with examinations of self- and student evaluation.

HUNGATE, T. L. *Management in Higher Education.* New York: McGraw-Hill, 1964.

HUNTER, J. O., "Faculty Evaluations as a Liberal Persuasion." *Improving College and University Teaching,* 1969, *17,* 90–92.

In developing any system of evaluation, decisiveness is not

so important as good faith. Especially in the community college still seeking its identity, a spirit of collegiality should obviate coercive methods. Seen in this light, evaluation is a matter for persuasion which emanates from a liberal base. The teacher expects that the system shall be enlightening and instructive rather than merely laudatory or abrasively critical. Four instruments for evaluation are suggested: student ratings, classroom visitation, a colleague relationship (senior and junior professor) on teaching, and an evaluation portfolio.

"Improving College Teaching." *School and Society*, 1968, *95*, 271–272.

The article discusses a program at the University of Colorado's School of Education in which professors are provided an opportunity to meet with Homer C. Rainey, professor emeritus of higher education. Dr. Rainey meets with one or two teachers a day to discuss their particular teaching problems. A monthly seminar is provided to facilitate discussion in this area.

Institute for Higher Education. *Student Evaluation of Teaching: Presentations at a Conference*. Pittsburgh, Pa.: University of Pittsburgh, 1970. 20 pp.

One paper by W. J. McKeachie, "Research on Student Ratings of Teaching," discusses his AAUP article on evaluation of teaching and, particularly, criticisms of it. He cautions that student evaluation of teaching can be valid but the ultimate purpose of evaluating teaching is to improve learning. Evaluation is not an end in itself. A second paper by George L. Fahey, "Student Rating of Teaching: Some Questionable Assumptions," concludes that student rating procedures are probably more objective, reliable, and perhaps valid than any alternative procedure we now use for

117

such assessment. The ratings procedures, however, should be carefully interpreted.

ISAACSON, R. L., AND OTHERS. "Correlation of Teacher Personality Variables and Student Ratings." *Journal of Educational Psychology,* 1963, *54,* 110–117.

Five personality factors—surgency, agreeableness, dependability, emotional stability, and culture—are generally described as relevant traits to teaching. The purpose of this study was to determine whether these personality traits can correlate with effective college teaching. The only high correlation achieved (0.48) was between the peer rating of culture and student ratings of effectiveness.

JENCKS, C., AND RIESMAN, D. The Academic Revolution, Garden City, N.Y.: Doubleday, 1969.

JOHNSON, J. A. "Instruction: From the Consumer's View." In C. B. T. Lee (Ed.), *Improving College Teaching.* Washington, D.C.: American Council on Education, 1967.

KARMAN, T. A., "Faculty Evaluation." *Liberal Education,* 1969, *55,* 539–544.

The article describes the new faculty evaluation system developed for Defiance College. The system incorporates three decision-making levels on faculty performance—the dean, division chairman, and the students. In the spring, the division chairman and the dean submit progress reports evaluating each teacher in seven areas: classroom effectiveness, student relations in general, constructivity regarding college programs, ability to work with other faculty members, committee effectiveness, administrative effectiveness, and community relations. (Not all categories apply to each person.) The student uses a five-point scale for judging teach-

118

ing effectiveness. Strengths and weaknesses and a plan for dealing with the latter are developed for each instructor.

KENT, L. "Student Evaluation of Teaching." *The Educational Record*, 1966, *47*, 376–406.

The American Council on Education Survey of 1966 found that in only one institution in ten are systematic student ratings used in all or most departments. Such ratings are not used at all in 48 per cent of the institutions surveyed. Those who have seriously examined the question of student evaluation feel that students are very perceptive and that ratings are not affected by such factors as rater's or teacher's sex, class size, or grade-point average. Students do tend to be overly lenient in their ratings, particularly in cases where the administration conducts the program and requires evaluation of all its faculty members.

KERLINGER, F. N. "Student Evaluation of University Professors." *School and Society*, October 1971, *99*, 353–356.

An analysis is made of student evaluations of professors and their teaching. The central point is that such evaluations are not an integral part of the instructional process and thus alienate professors, causing instructor hostility and resentment, undermining professional autonomy, diminishing professional motivation, and eroding professional responsibility. The article supports responsible evaluation of instruction— that which is initiated and conducted by professors as part of instruction.

KERR, C. "Destiny—Not So Manifest." In G. K. Smith (Ed.), *New Teaching, New Learning: Current Issues in Higher Education 1971*. San Francisco: Jossey-Bass, 1971.

KIRCHNER, R. P. "A Control Factor in Teacher Evaluation by Students." Unpublished research paper. Lexington, Kentucky: College of Education, University of Kentucky, 1969. 7 pp.

The purpose of this research study was to determine whether the individual administering an evaluation instrument has any significant effect on the results, and which evaluation is most representative of the students' real evaluation of the teacher. This study, involving 10 sections and 227 students in an introductory educational psychology course, found a significant difference (at .05 level) between whether or not the instructor or a neutral individual administered the student evaluation form. Higher ratings were achieved when the instructor administered the survey.

LANGEN, T. D. F. "Student Assessment of Teaching Effectiveness." *Improving College and University Teaching,* 1966, *14,* 22–25.

Forty-three years of assessing student opinion of teaching at the University of Washington has resulted in the current survey form of ten items. Analyses of these forms indicate that there is no relationship between the rating received by the instructor and the grade the student expects to receive from the course. System of rating has merit, but the same items should not be used for all disciplines and for all levels of instruction.

LAURITS, J. "Thoughts on the Evaluation of Teaching." *The Evaluation of Teaching.* Washington, D.C.: Pi Lambda Theta, 1967.

Discusses some of the problems associated with evaluation at various levels. Explains that the school has a responsibility to the student. The main burden of the evaluation of teaching must rest with the teachers—the process should become a part of the teaching process itself. Model schools or pilot institutions can be designated to study evaluation methods and procedures.

LEE, C. B. T. (Ed.) *Improving College Teaching*. Washington, D.C.: American Council on Education, 1967. 407 pp.

The book centers around and comments on eight papers prepared for the American Council on Education. The work is essential for those interested in evaluation, particularly Part 4 on "Teaching and Learning," and Part 5 on "The Evaluation of Teaching Performance."

LEHMANN, I. J. "Evaluation of Instruction." In P. Dressel (Ed.), *Evaluation in Higher Education*. Boston: Houghton Mifflin, 1961.

A list of specific suggestions on teaching aids will not necessarily improve the degree of instruction or learning. Calls for more appraisal of individuals before hiring and abolishment of the practice of talking about teaching and paying for something else. Added attention needs to be focused on experimentation with instructional processes and appraisal of how teaching affects students.

LEWIS, E. C. "An Investigation of Student-Teacher Interaction as a Determiner of Effective Teaching." *Journal of Educational Research*, 1964, *57*, 360–363.

The purpose of the investigation was to determine whether students and teachers tend to interact along measurable personality dimensions. Three groups of students were chosen: the first two groups provided a control of sex (male) and variation of subject matter, while the third group provided a variation of sex. Each student, as well as selected instructors in various fields, completed two questionnaires—The Guilford-Zimmerman Temperament Survey, and a one hundred-item biographical inventory. The results did not support the hypothesis. It was also concluded that effective teachers cannot be differentiated from less effective teachers on the basis of personality variables.

121

LOCKSLEY, N. "A Mathematical Look at Evaluation of Teaching." *School Science and Mathematics,* 1967, *67,* 797–798.

The purpose of this experiment was to see how difficult it would be to mathematically develop some exact measure of teaching performance. What the observer hopes he is evaluating—teaching performance—is actually the sum of teaching ability, environmental influence on teaching, bias toward the person, bias toward the field, and two random errors—errors in teaching performance and errors in observation. The author concluded that the problems of evaluation seem too complex for mathematical measurement.

LORGE, I. "The Fundamental Nature of Measurement." In E. F. Linquist (Ed.), *Educational Measurement.* Washington, D.C.: American Council on Education, 1951.

LUNDSTEDT, S. "Criteria for Effective Teaching." *Improving College and University Teaching,* 1966, *14,* 27–31.

Discusses the point that teaching is basically communication. Criteria essential to good teaching and related to communication are: knowledge of one's subject matter, empathy, and sense of timing. Proper timing is the most difficult to achieve in class. The effective communicator is generally the effective teacher.

MC KEACHIE, W. J. "Research in Teaching: The Gap Between Theory and Practice." In C. B. T. Lee (Ed.), *Improving College Teaching.* Washington, D.C.: American Council on Education, 1967.

MC KEACHIE, W. J. "Student Ratings of Faculty." *AAUP Bulletin,* 1969, *55,* 439–444.

Increased interest in college teaching seems to be reflected in increased demands for ways of evaluating teaching. In spite of the somewhat spotty evidence on the validity of student evaluations of teaching, their use is increasing. That "feed-back" or "knowledge of results" aids learning is a psycho-logical principle of long standing. Used with other "feed-back" devices, student evaluations may be of much value to teachers. (The article also includes a form for student eval-uation of teaching.)

MC KEACHIE, W. J., AND OTHERS. "Student Ratings of Teacher Effectiveness." *American Educational Research Journal,* 1971, *8,* 435–445.

The validity of student ratings of teaching effectiveness was assessed in five studies. Ratings of teachers on the "skill" factor were positively related to mean achievement in four of the five studies but not as consistently for men as for women. Women teachers rated high in "structure" were more effective than men. Teachers rated high on "rapport" were effective on measures of student thinking. Teachers rated as having an impact on beliefs were effective in chang-ing attitudes.

MC NEIL, J. D. "Concomitants of Using Behavioral Objectives in the Assessment of Teacher Effectiveness." *The Journal of Ex-perimental Education,* 1967, *36,* 69–74.

The data provide evidence that the emphasis and use of operational definitions of instructional goals, including speci-fication of criterion measures, in the supervisory process is accompanied by more favorable assessment of teachers by supervisors and greater gain in desired directions on the part of learners.

MARTIN, T. W., AND BERRY, K. J. "The Teaching-Research Di-lemma: Its Sources in the University Setting." *The Journal of Higher Education,* 1969, *40,* 691–703.

The authors contend that professors are caught in an inter-positional role conflict: teach for the university or publish for the profession. The university hires a professor mainly to teach, but retains or promotes him very largely on the basis of his scholarship. The authors advocate a separation of research and teaching functions as a way of resolving the inherent role conflict.

MAYHEW, L. B. "A Tissue Committee for Teachers." *Improving College and University Teaching,* 1967, *15,* 5–10.

While most professions have evolved means by which the effectiveness of practice can be judged (i.e. pathological tissue committee in medicine), only college teaching seems to have exempted itself from any kind of realistic assessment. Sequentially, the evaluation process consists of formulating broad educational purposes or objectives, specifying them into discrete behavioral terms, seeking appropriate relevant learning experiences, accumulating evidence of successful or unsuccessful demonstration of desired behaviors, and, finally, making judgments as to whether or not the broad educational objectives have been achieved.

The four reasonable sources for evidence concerning teaching are the teacher himself, the student, someone who has seen teaching in progress, and demonstrations of behaviors which the teaching was intended to modify.

MEDLEY, D. M., AND MITZEL, H. E. "Measuring Classroom Behavior by Systematic Observation." In N. L. Gage, (Ed.), *Handbook of Research on Teaching.* Chicago: Rand McNally, 1963.

The proper role of direct observation in research on teacher effectiveness would seem to be as a means of learning something about the teaching process and its relationship to pupil learning. The main purpose of this section in the AERA *Handbook* is to extract from a number of studies whatever can be learned that would be useful in planning future observational studies.

MEGAW, N. "The Dynamics of Evaluation." In C. B. T. Lee (Ed.), *Improving College Teaching*. Washington, D.C.: American Council on Education, 1967.

Contains opinions on the advantages and disadvantages of evaluating teaching effectiveness. The present methods of objective evaluation are regarded as so ineffective that the only solution may well be completely subjective evaluation by committee.

MEREDITH, G. M. "Dimensions of Faculty-Course Evaluation." *The Journal of Psychology,* 1969, *73,* 27–32.

The study sought to establish the dimensions of faculty-course evaluation. The Illinois Course Evaluation Questionnaire and A Student's Rating Scale of an Instructor were administered to 1097 students at the University of Hawaii. Sixty-seven variables were intercorrelated and factor analyzed, resulting in a nine-factor solution. Two of the factors, labeled "instructor impact" and "instructional impact," accounted for 64 per cent of the rotated variance. The findings were discussed in light of a systems approach to evaluation.

MITZEL, H. E. "Teacher Effectiveness." *Encyclopedia of Educational Research.* New York: The Macmillan Co. 1960.

MORTON, R. K. "Evaluating College Teaching." *Improving College and University Teaching,* 1961, *9,* 122–123.

Various types of evaluation are discussed. Student evaluations, in spite of limitations and faults, can be quite helpful. Improvisations can also take place, such as the students' verbal discussion of the good and the bad aspects of teaching in the last class period or a written critique. Administrative visitation evaluation should be done on more than one occasion and the evaluator should be supplied with course outline and be briefed in advance on course content, purposes, and procedures.

MORTON, R. K. "Student Views of Teaching." *Improving College and University Teaching*, 1965, *13*, 140–142.

Student evaluation of teachers is useful to the university administration, particularly to the academic dean, if it is used, along with other data, in evaluating a teacher's professional competence and teaching effectiveness in any given course and with a specific class. Proper allowance should be made for misinterpretation and possible frivolous or vindictive use by students.

MUSELLA, D., AND RUSCH, R. "Student Opinion on College Teaching." *Improving College and University Teaching*, 1968, *16*, 137–140.

Analysis of the 394 student responses at the State University of New York at Albany indicated that the teaching behaviors which most promote thinking, in order of importance, were: (1) attitudes toward subject; (2) attitudes toward students; (3) effective use of questions; (4) speaking ability; (5) knowledge of subject; (6) organization of subject matter; and (7) extensive and effective use of discussion. Expert knowledge of subject was chosen frequently by students as an important characteristic associated with effective teaching in general. Systematic organization of subject matter and ability to explain clearly were among the top three behaviors in the physical and biological sciences, but ability to encourage thought and enthusiastic attitude toward subject were among the top three for the arts and social sciences.

NEELEY, M. "A Teacher's View of Teacher Evaluation." *Improving College and University Teaching*, 1968, *16*, 207–209.

Teachers have been rated and evaluated since the beginning of teaching and may expect to be evaluated in the future. But there is not, even in this day of standardized tests, a new and objective way of evaluating teachers. There is lack of agreement among authorities as to what constitutes a good teacher. A review of the literature over the past twenty-five years indicates no objective usable criterion for identifying effective teachers.

NEWELL, D. *Evaluation of Teachers*. University of Kentucky: College of Dentistry Conference on Evaluation of Teaching and Teachers. Preconference readings, 1967.

Previous findings on the effectiveness of student evaluation of teaching are given. These studies investigated how ratings were obtained, if students qualified, and so forth. Conclusions indicate that: students are fairly good raters of their teachers; class size often affects ratings; only slight differences are evident in ratings for teachers of required and elective courses; students judge class procedures better than overall teaching ability; and in ranking instructors, degrees make a difference; and the quality of teaching in dental schools is good, but the need for improvement warrants serious consideration.

New Mexico State University. *Manual on the Explanation of Merit Rating System Rating Information Form*. Las Cruces, N.M., 1966.

New Mexico State University grants salary increases on a merit basis. Each faculty member fills out a form annually. The evaluation is based on three kinds of contributions: teaching, research and/or creative scholarship, and professional service. The assigned duty load is considered in the final rating. The department head and others concerned make judgments to the best of their ability with the information at their command. Factors considered in evaluating

127

teachers are: knowledge of subject matter; organization of material; attitude toward students; and attitude toward teaching. Points considered in connection with research and/or creative scholarship are: preparation; planning and execution; results; and direction of graduate students. Factors considered in evaluation of professional service are: service with students; committee work—department, college and university; and off-campus professional work. Department heads study the information form, confer with the faculty member concerning strengths and weaknesses, confer with the appropriate dean, and assign a rating.

OZMON, H. "Publications and Teaching." *Improving College and University Teaching,* 1967, *15,* 106–107.

All faculties, college and university, should be divided not only into departments but into two distinct sections within departments: one section for those who teach, and the other for those who do research and publishing, giving equal status to each, since one is no more important than the other. Thus a good teacher could become a full professor without publishing anything. The author also states that teacher self-evaluation is faulty: more weight should be placed on evaluation by students; faculty should be allowed to judge fellow staff members; and administrators need to be more energetic in evaluating teachers.

PERRY, R. R. *Criteria of Effective Teaching in an Institution of Higher Education.* Toledo, Ohio: Office of Institutional Research, The University of Toledo, 1969a. 17 pp.

PERRY, R. R. "Evaluation of Teaching Behavior Seeks to Measure Effectiveness." *College and University Business, 47,* 18. 1969b.

PHILLIPS, B. N. "The 'Individual' and the 'Classroom Group' as

Selected and Annotated Bibliography

Frames of Reference in Determining Teacher Effectiveness."
Journal of Educational Research, 1964, *58,* 128–131.

This study tests the hypothesis that teaching effectiveness,
determined by the uniform application of criteria, is different
from teaching effectiveness determined by selective application of criteria. In other words, teacher effectiveness is
measured by the extent to which what happens in the class
agrees with what the student wants. Results indicated that
students favored a highly structured class with "highly
visible" tests over a highly motivating class with a strong
emphasis on personal warmth. Additional evidence indicated
that student characteristics play a crucial role in the perception of teacher effectiveness.

POGUE, F. G., JR. "Students' Ratings of the 'Ideal Teacher.'" *Improving College and University Teaching,* 1967, *15,* 133–
136.

The evaluation form prepared by Quick and Wolf at the
University of Oregon was used to determine the "ideal
professor" at Philander Smith College. Forty-six per cent
(307 students) of the total college enrollment was polled.
Characteristics listed as most important were: good knowledge of subject (41%); a good evaluator (14%); explains
clearly (12%). Characteristics of the ideal teacher listed as
least important were: is scholarly and participates actively
in research (31%); likes college age youth (23%); has
adequate and well modulated voice (11%); and encourages
independent thinking.

PRIEST, B. J. "Classrooms: Castles or Learning Laboratories." In
C. B. T. Lee (Ed.), *Improving College Teaching.* Washington, D.C.: American Council on Education, 1967.

PUNKE, H. H. "Improvement in College Teaching." *Improving College and University Teaching,* 1965, *13,* 159–161.

As much objectivity as possible must be included in evaluation. Personal observations, interviews, opinionaires, analysis of learned judgments, and similar evaluative devices are most helpful when they lean toward the overall objective, and are used in relation to items listed on a point scale. The aims of a course, facilities, and conditions must be carefully considered in evaluative efforts.

RAYDER, N. F. "College Student Ratings of Instructors." *The Journal of Experimental Education,* 1968, *37,* 76–81.

A study of rating characteristics of 4285 college students at Colorado State College found that: students remembered and accurately reported their grade point averages; ratings of instructors were not substantially related to student's sex, grade level, major area, GPA or grade(s) previously received from the instructor; and instructors who differ on certain characteristics were rated differently by their students.

REMMERS, H. H. "Rating Methods in Research on Teaching." In N. L. Gage (Ed.), *Handbook of Research on Teaching.* Chicago: Rand McNally, 1963.

Rating scales should include these five properties: objectivity, reliability, sensitivity, validity, and utility. The section reviews genera and species of rating scales and their properties, and discusses and analyzes some issues and programs in research on teaching in which rating scales may be or have been applied. Rating scales are categorized in five major groupings: numerical, graphic, standard, cumulated-points, and forced-choice.

REMMERS, H. H., AND WEISBRODT, J. A. *Manual of Instructions for the Purdue Rating Scale for Instruction.* West Lafayette, Indiana: University Book Store, 1965. 17 pp.

This booklet, as well as the student response card and the

rating scale, summarizes one-third of a century of use of the Purdue Rating Scale. The Purdue Rating Scale is perhaps the most widely known scale; the bibliography in the manual begins with a 1927 entry. In addition, the manual outlines procedures for using available IBM equipment for computerized processing.

RENNER, R. R. "A Successful Rating Scale." *Improving College and University Teaching*, 1967, *15*, 12–14.

The students are the ultimate consumers of the teacher's efforts, and they know best whether he has been effective or not. They are not trained judges of the suitability of their mentor's methods, but they do judge whether or not the course had value for them. Although their reactions are not the only index of teacher competence, they appear to be most sharply focused on teaching itself, both its content and process. A college administrator usually evaluates teaching largely on the basis of casual reports from students and faculty members. With these factors in mind, a faculty-approved rating scale was devised, and is included.

ROVIN, S. (Ed.). *Evaluation of Teaching and Teachers.* University of Kentucky, College of Dentistry. Proceedings of the Faculty Conference, 1967.

Areas of discussion are student evaluation, peer evaluation, administration evaluation, alumni evaluation, and self-evaluation. Examination of reports in the various areas indicates the following: (1) student evaluation of subject matter competency should be viewed with caution; pedagogical skills are evaluated by students more easily, and professional attitudes and habits are the easiest areas for students to observe (relevance is questioned); (2) voluntary selection of peers was mentioned; secrecy was deplored; objectives of the technique were questioned; and the need of provisions to inform the administration of inadequate department chairmen was discussed; (3) a system of assistance and correction is needed for administrative evaluation instead of reward or punishment; the department chairman plays a critical role which must be defined; the dean should serve as appellate authority; (4) the utilization of conferences and questionnaires for alumni evaluation was explored; (5) self-evaluation should be a conscious process and utilized continuously; it should not be used, by itself, to justify monetary or academic rank advancements.

ROWLAND, R. "Can Teaching Be Measured Objectively?" *Improving College and University Teaching,* 1970, *18,* 153–157.

Each approach to evaluation has its place as well as its limitations and shortcomings. None will work effectively in an unfriendly atmosphere. That atmosphere will prevail only when assessment of instruction is regarded throughout the academic community as a means of accomplishing overall improvement rather than as a threat to individuals. Because of the nature of college teaching, its measurement can never be entirely accurate and objective, but with effort and cooperation from all involved, measurement can be made less haphazard and subjective than it is now.

RYANS, D. G. "Teacher Behavior Can Be Evaluated." *The Evaluation of Teaching.* Washington, D.C.: Pi Lambda Theta. 1967.

RYDER, S. "Evaluating the Teacher." *Improving College and University Teaching,* 1970, *18,* 272–274.

The article describes one teacher's experience with a narrative-type student appraisal of an English I course. Lessons for the teacher: don't expect too many ideas from students; at the risk of boring yourself, be a little redundant; not every misinterpretation or dropout is your fault; ask them for an evaluation early in the term when you can remedy some misunderstandings before it is too late.

SAMALONIS, B. "Ratings By Students." *Improving College and University Teaching*, 1967, *15*, 11.

It is the author's contention that student ratings should be available as a basis for faculty advancement.

SANFORD, N. *Where Colleges Fail.* San Francisco: Jossey-Bass, 1967.

SCHWARTZ, R. "Student Power—In Response to the Questions." *The Future Academic Community: Continuity and Change.* American Council on Education, Annual Meeting. Background papers, 1968.

Much student criticism reflects discontent with the style of teaching rather than course content. Dull lectures, perfunctory examinations, papers graded without substantive comment, lack of classroom discussion, and inaccessability of the professor all rank much higher on the list of student gripes than complaints about curriculum. Students are competent judges of lectures, discussions, and papers.

SHANE, H. G. "How Do They Rate You, Professor?" *National Education Association Journal*, 1965, *54*, 18–22.

Comments by over three hundred students from some twenty-one colleges and universities are discussed. In compiling these conversations on evaluation, the author selected individuals who had completed at least two years of study.

SHOBEN, J. E., JR. "Gimmicks and Concepts in the Assessment of Teaching." In C. B. T. Lee (Ed.), *Improving College Teaching*. Washington, D.C.: American Council on Education, 1967.

The author discusses three problems related to teacher evaluation. (1) Teaching is hard to evaluate because of the lack

133

of conceptual framework; analytic thought should be encouraged. (2) Because there is inadequate information on teaching and its evaluation, the "answers" are comparably inadequate. (3) Goals may be atttained more readily if an effort to reformulate teaching is undertaken as an intellectually interesting problem.

SHROCK, J. G. *Student Evaluation of Instruction*. University of Illinois, College of Dentistry. Fifth Annual Faculty Conference, 1964.

A description is given of processes and methods pertaining to student evaluation of instruction at the University of California School of Dentistry. Experimentation with the evaluation results is undertaken to develop improvement of instruction, curriculum planning, and as a means of communication among students, faculty, and administration. Processes and methods include: student-faculty liaison committee; rating scale for lecture course; rating scale for clinical/lab instructors; application of results (letter of recommendation, feedback to instructors, dean functions as counselor); and validity of student appraisal.

SILBER, J. L. Remarks at the 23rd Annual Meeting of the American Association for Higher Education. Chicago, 1968.

SIMPSON, R. H., AND SEIDMAN, J. M. *Student Evaluation of Teaching and Learning*. Washington, D.C.: American Association of Colleges for Teacher Education, 1962a.

A large number and variety of types of evaluative items are presented with the aim of helping the instructor devise his own evaluative tool.

SIMPSON, R. H., AND SEIDMAN, J. M. "Use of Teacher Self-Evaluative Tools for the Improvement of Instruction." *Improvement of*

Selected and Annotated Bibliography

Instruction in Higher Education, Report to The American Association of Colleges for Teacher Education, 1962b.

A list of seventeen teacher self-evaluation tools was prepared and distributed to the 487 representatives of AACTE. Requests for the questionnaire were so numerous that eventually 5,303 questionnaires were available for analysis. The highest ranked approach on the list was the "comparative check on your efficiency using one teaching approach vs. your efficiency using another approach." However, the item with the highest success ratio was "voluntary and continuing colleague discussions or seminars by instructors of a particular course." Conclusions drawn as a result of the study were: (1) The tools judged most successful for self-evaluation in terms of information gathering are teacher oriented rather than student oriented. (2) Lack of knowledge about the process of self-evaluation is a restraining factor. (3) The use of self-evaluative tools is dependent upon the subject matter field involved. (4) An extremely small fraction of college instructors react almost violently to any self-evaluation proposal.

SLOBIN, D. Y., AND NICHOLS, D. G. "Student Rating of Teaching," *Improving College and University Teaching,* 1969, *17,* 244–248.

Student rating of teaching commonly has met opposition and hostility from faculty; yet, after a few years of experience, most faculties have come to accept and even praise it. The article refutes these common objections to student rating: student ratings are influenced by variables irrelevant to teaching; student ratings reflect only the instructor's personality; students cannot evaluate the goals of teaching; a man should be judged by his peers; and over-emphasis on teaching has bad consequences.

SMART, R. C. *The Evaluation of Teaching Performance from the Point of View of the Teaching Profession.* Chicago: American Psychological Association Meeting. 1965.

Various positions, principles, and committee reports of the AAUP are given. In reviewing the work of the AAUP, it was found that no committee had been formulated specifically to study evaluation procedures. Previous association statements relate that freedom of teaching has to do primarily with the selection of topics to be covered in a given course. Evaluation of instruction may be done by the college administration, but is better done by colleagues, who are in a better position to judge the dignity, courtesy and temperateness of language, the patience, considerateness and pedagogical wisdom employed.

SMITH, R., AND FIEDLER, F. E. "The Measurement of Scholarly Work: A Critical Review of the Literature." *Educational Record,* 1971, *52,* 225–232.

A good evaluation of publications and research probably requires several criteria. The place and frequency of citation of the work seems to be least contaminated by such factors as the prestige of the scholar's university or the sheer number of papers published. Other factors studied, and found to be useful, were productivity, recognition, and journal quality.

SPAIGHTS, E. "Students Appraise Teachers' Methods and Attitudes." *Improving College and University Teaching,* 1967, *15,* 15–17.

The investigation sought to answer two questions: (1) Do high achieving students have more favorable perceptions of instructors' teaching methods than low achieving students? (2) Do high achieving students view the personal attitudes of college instructors more favorably than low achieving students? Two samples (293 students) were examined. Results indicated that students with both high and low grade-point averages thought there was too much emphasis on the lecture method. Both groups agreed that there was a general lack of independent study. The LA group felt that too much emphasis was being placed on mastery of the textbook while the above-average students favored greater use of audio-visual aids than those below-average. Above-average students wanted more essay examinations. The majority of the LA students perceived the typical college instructor as being impersonal, dictatorial, sarcastic, and lacking enthusiasm in his work, while few HA students saw instructors as having many undesirable personality traits.

STEWART, C. T., AND MALPASS, L. F. "Estimates of Achievement and Ratings of Instructors." *Journal of Educational Research,* 1966, *59,* 347–350.

The article gives results of a study in which a course and instructor information form was administered by 67 instructors teaching 54 courses to 1,975 students. Analysis of the questionnaires showed that of the students sampled, those expecting higher grades graded their instructors significantly higher than those expecting low grades. Freshmen viewed grading policies more favorably than did upperclass students. Further analysis indicated that instructors should consider reducing the complexity of their classroom presentation for freshmen and increasing the sophistication of their presentation for upper classmen.

UNIVERSITY OF OREGON. "Projected System for Publishing Ratings of Teachers." Unpublished memorandum. Eugene, Oregon. No date given.

After studying the problem of whether a system could be devised for publishing and distributing student ratings of a teacher against his will, the university made the following resolution: "Systematic survey of student reaction to courses and instruction at the university would be welcomed and faculty assistance would be provided if requested. Furthermore, any evaluation may be published against the will of any faculty member, provided the faculty member states his position before publication time."

VAN WAES, R. "Student Freedoms and Educational Reform." *Stress and Campus Response: Current Issues in Higher Education.* San Francisco: Jossey-Bass, 1968.

We need to listen to student complaints to determine the sources of their frustration and dissatisfaction. Students object to curriculum; they desire relevance, commitment, and leverage. They object to teaching methods. They reject "canned knowledge," "packaged formulae," "learning by fiat," and the lack of "genuine" dialog. If students can criticize and actually share in the governance of their colleges, there will be an opportunity to confront institutional problems in a context that is both less dramatic and less explosive, and probably more fruitful.

WERDELL, P. *Course and Teacher Evaluation.* Washington, D.C.: United States National Student Association, 1966.

Various methods for dealing with course and teacher evaluation are described. Included in material are evaluation forms, questionnaires, discussions, and positions.

WILSON, L. *The Academic Man.* New York: Oxford University Press, 1942.

WILSON, R. C., AND OTHERS. "Characteristics of Effective College Teachers as Perceived by Their Colleagues." Unpublished manuscript. Berkeley, Calif.: Center for Research and Development in Higher Education, 1969. 18 pp.

The purposes of this study were to explore some of the characteristics which faculty members ascribe to colleagues whom they regard as effective teachers; to develop scales for measuring those of the characteristics which might be useful in quantifying judgments of teaching effectiveness by colleagues; and to discover some of the relationships between these scales and other variables.

WINTHROP, H. "Worth of a Colleague." *Improving College and University Teaching,* 1966, *14,* 262–264.

In the evaluation of teaching, where colleague opinion is taken into consideration, the majority can label the nonconformist or aggressive teacher as incompetent and convince the administration to take action. Scholarship and publication are often evaluated by peer approval. A reputable scholar may find his work judged to be of poor quality by his colleagues when he is a member of a minority within a department. Much of the judging of a colleague's worth takes place behind the scenes. Decision-makers in an administrative hierarchy will frequently avoid a confrontation between the faculty members being judged and their judging peers.

WOODRING, P. "Must College Teachers Publish or Perish." *Educational Digest* 1964, *30,* 35–37.

One reason for the emphasis on publications is that the prestige of the university rests on the publications of the faculty. Administrative personnel, as well as department chairmen, have little knowledge of their faculty's teaching competencies, and through long tradition they seldom visit classrooms. However, they can read a man's publications. A balanced faculty is needed.

YAMAMOTO, K., AND DIZNEY, H. F. "Eight Professors—A Study on College Students' Preferences Among Their Teachers." *Journal of Educational Psychology,* 1966, *57,* 146–150.

Students' preferences for different types of college professors—administrator, socialite, teacher, and researcher—from each of two sources, education and arts and sciences, were studied. Three hundred college students responded to a Likert-type inventory of the eight types of college professors. Teacher, researcher, socialite, and administrator were preferred in that order, and education was preferred to arts and sciences as a source.

ZOLLITSCH, H. G., AND KAIMANN, R. A. "Should Students Evaluate Faculties?" *Educational Media,* 1970, *2,* 10–12.

A student opinion survey was tested on the Marquette University campus and provided reasonable insights into the professional effectiveness of the academician. The twenty-two-question instrument has four sections; preparation; presentation; demands upon the student; and personal characteristics. These surveys pointed out the need for some improvement. Based upon findings of shortcomings, a prescribed program for strengthening these areas could be worked out.

Index

141

Index

Index

143

Index

Index

145